Alice's Drive

D1567889

Alice Huyler Ramsey

Alice's Drive

Republishing
Veil, Duster, & Tire Iron

Alice Huyler Ramsey

Annotated by Gregory M. Franzwa

The Patrice Press
Tucson, Arizona

Copyright © 2005
Gregory M. Franzwa

All rights reserved.

Library of Congress Cataloging-in-Publication Data

Ramsey, Alice.
  Alice's drive: republishing veil, duster and tire iron / Alice Huyler
Ramsey ; annotated by Gregory M. Franzwa.
      p. cm.
  Republication of: Veil, duster, and tire iron. Pasadena, CA : Castle
Press, 1961. With the addition of notes and ca. 100 pages entitled
"Chasing Alice" which detail her entire route.
  Includes index.
  ISBN 1-880397-56-0
  1. United States--Description and travel. 2. Automobile travel--
United States. 3. Ramsey, Alice--Travel--United States. I. Ramsey,
Alice. Veil, duster, and tire iron. II Franzwa, Gregory M. III. Title.

E168.R175 2005
917.304'911--dc22

                                                            2005045824

The Patrice Press
PO Box 85639
Tucson, Arizona
1/800/367-9242
books@patricepress.com

To the two Jims,
Powell and Ranniger,
with affection

Contents

Foreword

I think it was about 1994 when I became aware of this remarkable book about an even more remarkable woman. The new Lincoln Highway Association had been formed in Ogden, Iowa, two years earlier and as soon as I learned that Alice Ramsey had crossed the nation in 1909, on many of the same roads that would become the Lincoln Highway in 1913, I wanted that book very badly.

Veil, Duster, and Tire Iron is now commanding upwards of $400 on eBay, but I was able to borrow a copy through library loan, and copied the pages. What a fascinating book that was! The writing was most professional, and I deduced that Alice Ramsey was a class act in every respect.

H. Nelson Jackson had made the first successful cross-country trip, San Francisco to New York, only six years earlier, and many others had duplicated the feat, from one direction or another, since that time. The first successful heavier-than-air powered flight had taken place in 1903 as well. America was viewing flight only as a novelty, but there was growing feeling that the makers and owners of horseless carriages were onto something.

By 1908 people were aware of the dawning of the automobile age, prompted by the publicity attending long-distance racing. The "Thomas Flyer," built in Buffalo, won the New York-to-Paris race on July 30 of that year, becoming the most famous automobile in America. (It is on exhibit to this day in the National Automobile Museum in Reno.)

The Model T Ford was introduced that year, to become the most popular automobile of all time, with more than fifteen million sold before introduction of the Model A in 1928.

But in 1909, only 155,000 Americans owned automobiles, out of a total population of 80 million people. There were 290 automobile manufacturers, most employing only a few people. Continuing publicity was needed to convince the nation that the era of the horse had to succumb to the era of horsepower.

At 3 P.M. on June 1, 1909, some 20,000 New Yorkers gathered in Manhattan to watch six vehicles cross the starting line of the first coast-to-coast race. With a Seattle destination, the automobiles (including two Model

T's) would travel the very route to be taken by Alice just nine days later—the Albany Post Road. The men drove west from Albany to the south shore of Lake Erie, but then continued south to St. Louis, then west through Denver and northwest to Seattle. Alice had a better idea. They both traveled to Albany to avoid the Alleghenies, but Alice joined the route of the future Lincoln Highway in Indiana and proceeded due west to San Francisco.

The so-called "Ocean-to-Ocean" trip was a race, and four of the cars made it to Seattle—the first being one of the Fords, on the road just twenty-three days.

Alice's trip wasn't a race. The purpose, as far as she was concerned, was to prove that a woman—a perfectly normal young mother—was capable of driving an automobile from coast to coast, without help from a man. And in fact, despite occasional hindrance from men.

That was the Maxwell party line, but it was a little short of the truth. Alice was indeed a highly skilled driver, which is why she was chosen to make the run in the first place. And not a bad mechanic, to boot.

But the Maxwell executives encouraged their dealers all along the route to guide Alice across America, and they did. Some pulled her out when she got stuck. She pulled some of them out when *they* got stuck. Whatever, it was a tremendous adventure and this wonderfully talented woman gave us a fine book chronicling it.

This is her story, considerably amplified from her modest publication of 1961. It has lost none of its charm in the ensuing forty-four years. More than just a fun book to read, it will fill the reader with warmth and admiration for this delightfully modest young adventurer. And possibly it will serve to inspire young readers of today, spurring them to great achievements of their own.

—Gregory M. Franzwa
March, 2005

1

New York City to Poughkeepsie, New York

"PHEW! NANCY, that was a long day!" I exclaimed, setting down my suitcase in the motel at Dwight, Illinois.

Nancy Cooper and I had left Everett 125 miles east of Pittsburgh, Pennsylvania, at seven-thirty in the morning by way of the toll roads across the remainder of that state, Ohio and Indiana. A dearth of accommodations after leaving the turnpike at Hammond, Indiana, forced us to continue beyond my usual driving hours and we kept on until 9 p.m. when we reached this little village at the junction of Routes 17 and 66. We were amazed to find that we had traveled 616 miles! That broke my record for a single day's drive.[1]

Back in 1909 when I was the first woman to cross the continent at the wheel of a motor car, my day's run was anywhere between 4 and 198 miles. In those days the roads were rugged trails, the car's springs were as stiff as those of a wagon, and the motor—Ah, the motor! The Maxwell "30" may not have been as fast or as comfortable as the modern automobile, but it was sturdy! That motor surmounted more difficulties than a modern driver can dream of—and never coughed. I'm still proud of that Maxwell engine![2]

June the ninth, 1909, was the actual date of the start of my historic automobile trek from New York to San Francisco. My husband's two sisters, Nettie Powell and Margaret Atwood, and a younger unattached friend, Hermine Jahns, were my companions.[3] As we loaded the various extras into the Maxwell, Nettie asked:

"Do you think we have everything we really need?"

"Well, to me, of course, the *most* important items are the tools and parts to repair any emergency breaks. I'm sure we won't forget the few clothes we can accommodate besides what we wear on our backs," was my quick retort.

Spooner & Wells Photo

A. L. Westgard behind Maxwell at 1930 Broadway (umbrella).

This adventure was surely not going to be a "style show" in the accepted meaning of the word. Judging from the *amount* in each wardrobe, it was only slightly above the Hottentot version of clothing: except that whatever item was in question, there was plenty of it. Skirts were very long and

2

mighty full, and the subject—like an exhausting course in college—was therefore "extremely well-covered."

The four of us set out from our homes in Hackensack, New Jersey, in the dark-green touring car.[4] Mother Ramsey, William Atwood (Maggie's husband), Berry Lewis and my husband followed in another Maxwell to the company salesroom at 1930 Broadway, New York, the official starting point of the transcontinental run.[5] A considerable number of spectators were already assembled, among whom we noticed several good friends, together with members of the Maxwell-Briscoe Company, newspapermen and photographers.

On the curb we spotted "Senator" W. J. Morgan, head of the Automobile Section of the *New York Globe*, an able editor who had created a great deal of activity on the subject of Better Roads. Behind the auto, looking over our equipment, with umbrella in hand, was A. L. Westgard. He was

Left to right: Jahns, Powell, Atwood, Ramsey in rubber ponchos at start.

known even this early as the Pathfinder for the AAA and had mapped out

3

many possible routes for future automobilists.[6] A third celebrity I was happy to see present was Mrs. Joan Newton Cuneo, driver of large racing cars.

By this time there was no longer even hope that we would have a pleasant day for our take-off.

It was *pouring rain!*

Fortunately the Maxwell's leatherlike pantasote top was already raised, but we thought it wise to don our rain apparel.[7] This consisted of some "real stuff!"—long rubber ponchos voluminous in girth, and with sleeves shirred at the wrist into elastic hems, covered all but the head. That part of the anatomy was encased in a rubber helmet (highly recommended for a fisherman or for a fireman on duty) which was entered through a cape-like flounce flowing down over the shoulders. The face section had a visor protecting the eyes from ordinary rain. If, perchance, the wind blew too—well, let's not tackle that point now!

Those garments were most effectual rain shedders but they certainly did nothing to enhance the human figure! We adventurers resembled a quartette of nuns—the last thing on earth Nettie would wish to be! When a news photographer wanted to take our pictures, Nettie and Hermine removed their helmets; Maggie turned her visor back, revealing the white edge of the lining, like a wimple; I posed in full regalia. Spooner and Wells and Nick Lazarnick took several views of us so clothed, in and out of the Maxwell.

While this was in progress William Atwood and Van Wells, officers of the Elks' Lodge of Hackensack, disappeared from the crowd, visited a nearby florist, and returned with four beautiful bouquets of pink carnations. These they bestowed upon us with a short presentation speech as farewell tokens of best wishes from the Lodge. Though the solicitude was deeply appreciated, we were not quite sure what to do with these ambassadors of their respect and esteem!

I am a subscriber to the policy expressed by Cornelia Otis Skinner, who says: "If you're going to go, *go!*" We were there to start a trip which was to bring me the distinction of being the first woman to drive an automobile from New York City to San Francisco. We had a job to do. So—let's get at it, I thought somewhat impatiently.

But no! More pictures—then some questions from the bystanders. Walking around and gazing at the scarcity of extra equipment, one inquirer said:

"Where are your guns?"

"We aren't carrying any," I responded.

"What about protecting yourselves?" came back at me.

"We're not afraid. Mr. Westgard says we're better off without guns." That was true. He had strongly advised that we take no firearms. "A dog, yes, if you like; but no guns." We prized his counsel highly as he and his wife had had extensive practical experience and knew whereof they spoke.

Another bystander then inquired, "And don't you have any pillows?"

"Pillows?" I echoed with perhaps a touch of scorn, "If one of us needs a pillow, I guess she'll have to board a train to the next stop!" This journey demanded a sturdy crew and no invalids were invited!

By this time the photographers had snapped enough views of the vehicle and of us to fill several Sunday pictorials and the hour was approaching ten. With the prospect of a rainy drive ahead we were becoming more than a trifle restive.

"I think we ought to get started," I said. There must have been something in my voice which signified I meant business, for the men immediately handed the drippy carnations to us as we mounted to our seats in the waiting automobile. Willing hands reached for the crank handle at the front end but, suddenly recalling that this was to be a women's expedition, I said, "Wa-a-it a minute! We'd better get *ourselves* started!"

Since the exit from the driver's seat was blocked by two spare tires, Nettie was obliged to descend. Crawling out into the rain once more, I was about to give the crank a whirl when one of the camera men rushed up with a "Just one more, Mrs. Ramsey."

I stopped momentarily to oblige, then gave the motor a yank and away she went![8] As the engine roared into accelerated speed, I hurried around to retard the throttle.[9] (I was brought up *not* to race an engine and could never tolerate its running madly above the required revolutions.) Making my way through the people, I gave my husband a really farewell kiss. Then, realizing I was keeping my partner of the front seat standing in the rain, I ran around and climbed quickly back into place.

Ah yes, those dripping carnations! What to do with them? For the present I must cling to my poor wet "pretties." Placing them on my rubber lap with a little pat of appreciation and a final wave to the waiting throng, I let in the clutch, the wheels began to turn, and we were off. The chains on the rear tires clanked with the first revolution of the wheels and we went on our way up Broadway with a huge Simplex automobile acting as our proud escort as far as 95th Street. From that point on, we were on our own.

Manhattan is a long island and it was several miles before we crossed the Harlem River at Spuyten Duyvil and came into the town of Yonkers.[10] Right up the main street and on through the many small villages we went— not too interesting a drive at any time and now darkened and gloomy because of the rain. Dobbs Ferry, Irvington and Tarrytown were pleasanter places with handsome estates along the sides of the Albany Post Road. Pocantico Hills, stately residence of the Rockefellers, lay to the east and we did not pass it. If we kept to the main route there was little chance of losing our way, since it was a fairly direct line from New York to the capital at Albany.

From time to time we could glimpse vistas of the massive cliffs of the Palisades on the opposite shore of the Hudson River, glowing in their summer greenery. On our side, however, as we entered Tarrytown,[11] our minds were centered on some form of refreshment. The rain was a chilly one for June so we were not the least bit cheered when the local druggist suggested an ice cream soda!

"Is that all you have to offer?" we inquired, more or less in a chorus.

"Well," said he, "that seems to be what most people want."

We shivered visibly, and then Hermine was the one who voiced the wishes of us all.

"How about some hot chocolate?"

The druggist looked a little distressed and perhaps even disgusted at the request, but replied reluctantly, "Oh, I guess I can make some of that."

Welcome news to our iced-up muscles and joints! We quickly settled for four large hot chocolates and set out again, fortified for the next period of chill.

Since we had seen several Maxwell-Briscoe men in New York we were unprepared for others at Tarrytown. A few blocks beyond the drugstore stood a red Maxwell touring car containing three men—Mr. Coler and Mr. Bender of the official staff and the Company's photographer, shielding his camera from the inclement weather with a large black raincloth. They announced they would precede us for a few miles in order to get some views of our oncoming vehicle. The photographer stood in the rear of their automobile alone and, as the machine slid about on the gluey road, he created an hilarious sight, clutching his camera madly and trying to get what shots he could in transit. This piece of the Post Road had been oiled a short time before the rain and it was now extremely difficult to maintain one's course on it. We were laughing at his antics most of the time, so any results he achieved must at least have looked cheerful.

Finally the increasing downpour discouraged the three so completely that they decided they had had enough. Accordingly, they pulled into an entrance driveway and waited for us to come alongside.

"Well," said Mr. Coler, "I guess this is as far as we will go. The weather gets worse instead of better and we have a few shots which may pan out. Good luck to you and so long!"

We speculated on our chances for improved conditions and concluded we might as well accept the philosophy of the old colored man who said: "Kind of weather what we has is all we's gwine ter git."

Ossining was just ahead.[12] The forbidding buildings of Sing Sing Prison lay along the waterfront. This was the old-time type of jail, with the lock step and work on the rock pile. The very sight of it seemed sinister. Even so, it would take more than a prison to rob us of the appetite we, by then, had acquired. The eagerness with which we downed coffee and roast beef sandwiches at a nearby lunch counter would have convinced an onlooker we were eating our farewell meal prior to execution!

The rain continued to play an intermittent rat-a-tat drumming tune upon the pantasote top and I exclaimed:

"Drat the rain! Why can't it stop? Here we are in some truly historic country and I wanted to point out some special places. We can't see anything in this dreadful downpour!"

From here to Poughkeepsie we lapsed into a sort of coma. Probably some of us were thinking over the significance of the early history of our nation; perhaps we were just weary of the rain.[13] But I'm sure, by now, we all looked forward to being in a warm hotel where we could be comfortable and relax.

The distance from New York to our first night stop was very small by modern standards; but with the unimproved roads made so slippery by the storm, the 76 miles were plenty. Our arrival at the edge of town, however, revived us with anticipation. As we advanced into the village I was happy to glimpse again scenes which had become familiar and beloved while I was at Vassar College.

"You girls rest and do what you like. I believe I'll look up some of my former college mates." Let's see, I mused to myself, who's around now? When I really got down to figuring, most of them had gone two years before. Suddenly I felt deserted and alone in this well-known spot. Even the thought depressed me so much that the impulse to contact anyone left me as quickly as it had come.

So—instead of going to college—we all went to bed![14]

Notes

1. Alice never lost her love for long-distance driving, having made more than thirty trips coast-to-coast. She is describing one of those trips. She was born Nov. 11, 1886, in Hackensack, N.J. Her father, John Huyler, owned a coal and lumber business there.

2. A new 1909 Maxwell DA was delivered to Alice in Hackensack on May 12, 1909. It had a four-cylinder, thirty horsepower engine. The sticker price was $1,500 but it was a loaner from the manufacturer. The car probably was built at their Tarrytown, N.Y., factory.

3. Alice was 22; Hermine, 16; Nettie was 49; and Maggie was a few years younger.

4. Alice, her lawyer-husband John Rathbone Ramsey and their baby, John, born in 1907, lived in Hackensack, N.J. Her son died in 2000. A daughter, Alice, was born in 1910 and now lives in Florida.

5. Lincoln Center was built across Broadway from the site of the Maxwell showroom, 1930 Broadway. A new high-rise apartment building is now at the site of the dealership, replacing an earlier apartment tower.

6. A. L. Westgard, dubbed the "Pathfinder" of the American Automobile Association, was one of the earliest automobile travelers of the American West. In 1909, the AAA was just five years old.

7. Pantasote Co. produced a waterproof fabric, similar to but more flexible than leather. The company was headquartered in New York City in 1909, and has operated in Passaic, N.J., in recent years.

8. Engines of early automobiles, lacking a self-starter, were started by a crank, a front extension of the driveshaft. There was a technique to doing this. If the thumb was placed over the crank handle and the engine backfired, a broken arm could result. Experienced automobilists of the day would keep the thumb alongside the fingers when cranking.

9. The Maxwell DA had a throttle lever on the right side of the steering column, and a spark control lever on the left. With either an electric starter or a hand crank, the left lever was moved up to retard the spark, and the right lever down to advance the throttle. As soon as the engine started, the driver would lower the left lever to advance the spark and maximize power; while the right lever was moved upward to return the accelerator to the idle position. (The danger of backfiring while cranking was lessened if the spark was retarded.)

10. Alice was driving north on Broadway, the Albany Post Road, now close to or on US 9. She would have crossed the Harlem River on the Broadway Bridge, about nine miles to the north. Spuyten Duyvil (Dutch for spitting devil) is on the Henry Hudson Parkway, about a half-mile northwest of the Broadway Bridge. Yonkers had a population of about 78,000 in 1909.

11. US 9 goes through the center of Tarrytown today, as the Albany Post Road did in 1909.

12. The route is not signed as Broadway here, but Alice was on US 9 through Ossining.

13. The American history in this area is dramatic. George Washington stood on the Jersey shore and watched the British brutalize the captured Revolutionary forces on the west bank. Pre-revolutionary mansions still stand on the east bank—confiscated by colonists who suspected the owners of pro-Toryism. Beyond Tarrytown is Sleepy Hollow Cemetery, which holds the body of Washington Irving. A new bridge crooses Mill Brook, across which Ichabod Crane rushed when pursued by Irving's Headless Horseman. Not far to the north lived Katerina Van Tassel, a real person who was the object of the fictional Ichabod's affections.

14. Poughkeepsie would have been entered on Market Street, then and now US 9. The Nelson House was one of the leading hotels in 1909. Alice was in Vassar's class of 1907, but left school at the end of her sophomore year.

2

Remembering the Montauk Triumph

WHAT STARTED this transcontinental jaunt anyway?

How did I ever happen to become involved in such an adventure?

Carl Kelsey definitely put the idea into our heads one evening as we were dining at Montauk Point on Long Island, New York, after completing the first day of an endurance run in which I was driving my 1908 Maxwell red runabout.[15] He arose from the table and said:

"Mrs. Ramsey, I hope I have not caused you too much uneasiness today. I'm sure I must have appeared to stare at you for I have been thinking very deeply about the greatest promotional idea of my career. You know, I've driven Maxwells up stairways and attracted so much attention to them that they are about the best-known automobile in the world...But today I've thought of something that puts all the rest in the shade. I've watched you drive all day and I think you're the greatest natural woman driver I've yet seen. Now..."

Here Kelsey hesitated a moment, then continued, "Do you know what I am about to prophesy?"

Suddenly presented with this bewildering question, I was embarrassed and my tongue clung to the roof of my mouth. My face felt like a fireball and I would gladly have disappeared under the table. Yet I thought his question should be answered and I managed to emit a scarcely audible and very weak "No, Mr. Kelsey, I don't."

He looked at each of the people seated at the table, raised one arm and, pointing at me, went on:

"You are going to be the first woman ever to drive an automobile across the United States of America, from Hell Gate on the Atlantic to the Golden Gate on the Pacific…and in a Maxwell!"[16]

By now I was numb all over. He might as well have said I would fly to the moon the following week!

The Montauk Point Run had started outside New York City and went 150 miles to the lighthouse at the eastern tip of Long Island which stretches out into the Atlantic Ocean.[17]

Carl Kelsey was Sales Manager of the Maxwell-Briscoe Company in Tarrytown, N.Y., and a "natural" for seeing opportunities in special advertising stunts for the promotion of sales. His foresight was miles ahead of mine, and when I first heard his pronouncement I thought he must be—well, maybe a *little* crazy! But he had planted the seed of an idea and it certainly fell on fertile soil!

I was flabbergasted by the proposition. This was a challenge, if I ever had one. It sounded like a magnificent adventure and—I liked it. But a lot was involved. Would my husband even hear of it, would he approve, and if so, who would go?

On the drive back to New York there was opportunity to think over the pros and cons of the suggested journey. I recall a large County Fair at Riverhead where we had luncheon and where we received enthusiastic applause as the autos paraded in line around the grounds.

From time to time Nettie or Maggie would make some inquiry regarding the future adventure. Since I had often heard them say they would not go to Europe I considered them unlikely candidates for so lengthy a trip. It turned out that it wasn't the long trek but fear of the water that prevented even the germ of a desire for ocean travel lodging in the mind.

"Do you think you would like to drive all the way to California?" asked Nettie. She didn't seem to disbelieve it so much as to be testing my attitude toward the matter.

"Why not?" said 1, "if Bone wouldn't object to my going. It's been done by men and as long as they have been able to accomplish it, why shouldn't I?"[18]

Maybe my remark showed more spunk than common sense; but, at 21, perhaps that's to be expected.

More miles intervened. The highlight of the Montauk Run seemed to have passed with the close of the first day. But we had to return to New York so we just plugged along.

Later Maggie piped up, "We won't be able to carry much luggage, will we? And how will we dress for it?"

So-o-o, she was evidently thinking rather seriously of being part of the adventure!

My mind, too, was busy with prospects of the future.

Nettie and Maggie were well into their forties, Nettie the older by several years, while I was in my early twenties. The "girls," as we referred to my husband's sisters, well-groomed and dressed in the daintiest of French-heel footgear, were conservative and reserved to the nth degree. Nettie assumed a sort of dominance in decisions; Maggie was the more submissive and sensitive type. Nettie would pursue her show of authority as far as she could maintain it, unless gently reproved by Mother.[19] And Maggie took it in peace.

Because of our age difference I felt considerable awe in their presence and refrained from expressing my opinion where it might run counter to theirs. How was it going to work on a trip of such length with these two sisters? Could such dressy and fastidious women manage with little in the way of fancy clothes for so long a period? And would they accept the privations of a rugged jaunt across more or less uncharted country? What about food? Would they trust my decisions in regard to the automobile and its handling?

This debate kept racing back and forth through my mind as we drove back to the city. By the time we reached home it was apparent the girls were not only willing but eager to participate in the adventure and I was happy to include them in the "crew." So, with the encouragement of their backing, I broached the subject to my husband, acquainting him first with the way the challenging suggestion had come to us.

More than twice my age and with many years of experience as a counselor-at-law and county official, Bone was a recognized political figure of considerable stature. Although he was better qualified than I to pass on matters concerning us, nevertheless he kept an open mind, allowed me to hold an independent opinion, and never "fenced me in." But how could we know what effect this daring project of his dear ones driving into almost unknown parts of our land would have upon him? I am sure he never understood *why* we wanted to go on this long trek but the fact that we did was reason enough for him. He had implicit confidence in us even if he didn't understand or share the desire.

We need not have feared his final decision or been nervous about it, for soon he said, "Well, if Nettie and Maggie want to go with you, I'm willing." That was a hurdle behind us!

Shortly thereafter we learned of another automobile reliability run, for women drivers only, from New York to Philadelphia. The idea of such an event was derided in some newspapers as dangerous and ridiculous and beyond the capabilities of women drivers. This criticism, of course, merely whetted the appetites of those of us who were convinced that we could drive as well as most men. Each driver was allowed one passenger, a "mechanician," and I had chosen as my companion Hermine Jahns, who had recently come from Wisconsin to live with her sister, Mrs. Boettger, in Hackensack. We had a wonderful two days of motoring fun with all the other feminine auto enthusiasts and carried off one of the trophies with a perfect score. It was only natural that this association would result in Hermine being the logical fourth on the transcontinental trip if her family were willing she should go. After several conferences, they gave their consent and our quartette was complete.

From that time our chief activity was preparing for the start of the trip set for early June. The Maxwell-Briscoe Company generously furnished the automobile and agreed to pay the actual expenses of the journey. Its officers also instructed their agents to keep on hand tires, gasoline and spare parts in case of any breakdowns, and asked that their representatives give us every possible attention, Most of them did just that, some even entertaining us in their homes. We made many good friends whom we cherish to this day.[20]

Because of the great distances between places in the west, it was thought advisable to install a 20-gallon fuel tank instead of the regular 14-gallon one. There was also a rack for two extra tires on the right side of the vehicle with a circular drum-like trunk in the open space, in which we could store spare tubes and a tire repair kit. As it was foreseen there might well be instances when we would be unable to reach the next food or overnight stop as scheduled, the company provided a picnic hamper with a minimum of food rations and eating equipment, and a camera which took photos of post-card size. At the beginning of our trip this just about comprised our entire equipment; in the West we added a few things for emergencies.

As to our personal needs, the subject of clothes was a *very* important item. We figured we could have but one suitcase apiece and, since automobiles then had no provision for luggage, it would be necessary to have a carrying rack attached to the rear of the vehicle. Maybe in the early motoring days when roads were so terrible, people were not supposed to wander far enough from home to *need* a suitcase! But these four cases had to be accommodated somewhere and there was not that much extra room *inside* the auto. To protect them from the weather enroute they were wrapped each morning in a rubber cloth and removed each afternoon on arrival at our destination wet, dusty, or muddy according to the vicissitudes of the weather.

One suitcase is a small allowance for a woman in days when there was no such thing as nylon—(bless its little traveling heart!) so we had to plan our clothes most carefully. Into the cases went our "city duds"—dressy suits with pretty blouses, an extra pair of good-looking shoes, and the usual change of underwear and overnight necessities. Dresses were long and full in that era, so this amount just about filled a case. Nettie and Maggie both owned beautiful traveling luggage, fitted with cut-glass containers with silver tops for toilet articles. Hermine and I, young things that we were, were not so richly blest and even if we had such, I think we would have left them at home for an easier trip.

For day-by-day wearing we had chosen suits of tan covert cloth as being most practical as far as dust and light rain were concerned. With those we wore simple blouses, dusters in warm and dry weather, and for rain, rubber ponchos and hats. Our fair-weather hats were a type of large full cap with stiff visors to shield the eyes in the low western sun, over which crepe de chine veils were draped and came under the chin to be tied in billowing bows.

In the light of more recent years this 1909 Maxwell "30" touring car was of sturdy construction, high off the ground, with a running-board on either side—the intermediate step between the floor of the automobile and the ground. The driver occupied the right front seat, since the vehicle was

14

then built with a right-hand drive, and controlled the gear shift and the emergency brake levers with the right hand. There were 4 gears arranged in progressive order: reverse (far forward), then neutral position, and three forward speeds. Also at the right hand just beside the seat was the rubber bulb of the "honk-honk" horn. The presence of the spare tires on the right side precluded egress from the driver's seat, which I mentioned before.

The spark and gasoline throttle levers were located beneath the steering wheel, on the steering post. On the dash was a nonvibrating coil, an odometer (early name for speedometer) and a glass tube through which one could view the circulation of the oil.[21] The crank with which the engine was started remained permanently fixed to the front of the auto. The motor received its initial impulse from dry cell batteries and the current was then switched over to the magneto. (My previous 1908 Maxwell ran on a storage battery only.) The fuel tank was located under the front seat and its contents had to be approximated by measuring with a ruled stick. There was no gasoline gauge at that time.[22]

On the left running board was a carbide generator for making illuminating gas for the headlamps and a metal tool box large enough to contain the hand pump and other tools. These were placed so as to leave sufficient space between them to permit the passengers to get in or out of the vehicle. There were no bumpers then in vogue on the front and rear ends. Motorists were moderate enough in their driving habits to maintain safety without that assistance!

The four cylinders of the motor were individually cast and water-jacketed. There were two sets of brakes on the rear wheels, one external contracting and the other internal expanding. They sufficed for the top speed of the auto, not much over 40 miles per hour. Something all motor cars had in 1909 which has been largely eliminated in the present day is the sheet metal pan beneath the motor. This was a protection from road damage.

The weight of the transcontinental Maxwell, without load, was 2100 pounds.

A good car; but what kind of driver?

I was born mechanical, an inheritance from my father. As I grew up I showed great curiosity about the working of any device and by the time I was almost out of grade school I had elected to take manual training instead of some feminine art. My father, who had magic in his fingers, understood my interests and encouraged me.

My husband wasn't mechanical at all; but in his own way, he encouraged me too. I didn't even ask for the shining red Maxwell that was delivered to our door as a gift from him. It was a roadster with two "bucket" seats in front and a fold down "jump" seat in the rear. It was upholstered in red tufted leather and was a mighty pretty sight. Billy Wood of the local agency was assigned to teach me to drive.

Going up Passaic Street that first day I veered to escape hitting a small dog which had appeared suddenly in the path of the auto. At this Billy said, "Mrs. Ramsey, never, never turn aside to miss a dog. You might hit a pole and kill yourself." I still think of that advice, though I'd hate to hurt an animal. But he had something there.

On the morning scheduled for the second lesson, Billy telephoned and said he was obliged to go to Pelham Manor. Of course I was disappointed. When he shyly added, "Unless you want to go along," I was rather surprised, until I realized he intended that to serve as the lesson. Then I asked, "In my car?" to which he replied in the affirmative. When he picked me up he remarked he would have to make a stop downtown and did I want to drive that far. Did I!

When he emerged from Halstead's Bazaar, the local hardware "emporium," he enquired, "Do you feel like driving farther?"

I assented with enthusiasm. I was loving every minute of it and gaining confidence fast. So down Main Street we went, over the Court Street Bridge, proudly past my father's coal office, on up the Bogota hill on Fort Lee Road, mile after mile, and finally down the steep snake-like Fort Lee Hill onto the ferry to uptown New York.[23] On the boat we were sandwiched between horses and wagons. Well, I expected every minute he would take the wheel. At last, when I had driven all the way to Pelham Manor through the streets of upper New York City and then back again to Hackensack, it was certain I needed no more teaching to drive that automobile! I admit I was tired—not enough to relinquish the wheel of my own accord on the way—but I was buoyed up by the accomplishment. Not bad for the second lesson! Traffic was light, I will say; but there was a lot of gear changing.

I was now completely enamored of this modern form of transportation and during the summer months I ticked off 6000 miles of pleasure driving, with my friends. We explored the highways around New Jersey, most of which were in the dirt stage or, in some cases, bound with crushed stone into macadam.

By the time we learned of the run to Montauk Point—that fateful trip that started me on the transcontinental tour—my husband's two sisters were anxious to participate for the fun of it. But not Bone! He never wanted to drive a car, although he was very generous in providing me with new automobiles in frequent succession. He always took one ride in each new automotive arrival. As soon as he was settled in the seat (if you can call it "settled") he always asked, "How do you stop this thing?" No, the Montauk Run was surely not for him so we invited Berry Lewis, the local Maxwell agent, to ride with us.

Hackensack was about fifteen miles out of New York, so we planned to leave at 4:30 a.m. to meet with some of the autos at Columbus Circle and proceed to Lynbrook, Long Island, the official starting point.[24]

Dressed in veil, goggles and duster, I climbed into my beautiful chariot with its high seats, righthand steering wheel, and windshield hinged in the middle. Since it was not daylight the oil lamps at the side and rear had to be lighted. We would also need the headlights so I dropped the carbide pellets into the gas generator on the running board and turned the cock to drip water upon the carbide. Then, opening the front lenses of the large lamps, I struck a match and applied the flame to the escape orifice. The odor of that gas was an indescribably acrid one.[25]

Cranking the engine was always part of the motoring adventure. It was a clash with an unpredictable temperament; a gamble with a possible broken arm. Give the crank a preliminary test, a decisive upward pull, listen for the rewarding cough and roar, then race to the steering post, advance the spark and retard the gas lever.

I backed out of the garage and curved my way backwards about 100 feet to the street.

Maggie and Nettie were waiting as I drew up before their house and Berry Lewis, who had walked down to meet us, climbed in beside me. Away we went to Lynbrook and the Montauk Run.

For several weeks the newspapers had been describing the preparations for the "pathfinders" to go the entire distance to the Montauk Point Lighthouse. Considerable attention had been paid to Mrs. Joan Newton Cuneo who was to drive a 50-horsepower Rainier, and to me with my smaller Max-

The three Maxwells on Montauk run, 1908. Left-hand car, Kelsey, Alfred Reeves, Bob Clothier, not known; middle car, Alice H. Ramsey, Berry Lewis, Mrs. Powell, Mrs. Atwood; right car, not known.

well, for we were the only women to attempt the run. As the vehicles gathered we noticed among the heavier type the Chalmers-Detroit, an Italian Zust and then, in marked contrast, a tiny Brush runabout. Much notoriety had been given to the new Model T Ford manufactured by Henry Ford in Detroit, but it had not yet been seen in New York. One of them was said to be entered in this run but there was no sign of it at Columbus Circle. We had heard also that there would be three Maxwells in the tour, so we looked forward to finding the others at Lynbrook.

Many residents stopped along the streets and watched us pass. We were quite surprised that they would find interest in our small parade, accustomed as they must have been to the more spectacular motor cars and crowds of the Vanderbilt Cup Races. There was, of course, great curiosity regarding this recent form of transportation and whenever people could get a glimpse of an automobile they were completely agog.

Arrived at Lynbrook, we discovered two other Maxwell models. A young man about thirty years of age jumped from the driver's seat in one of them and advanced toward us. He held out his hand in greeting to each of us and said, "I'm Carl Kelsey."

Kelsey had the opportunity only to say, "Let's keep the Maxwells together," before the flagman waved us on. Mrs. Cuneo's big Rainier, a little Reo, a Mora, a Haynes and a large Pullman touring car pulled ahead and we fell in behind the other Maxwells and headed for Freeport, Amityville, Bayshore and Blue Point.

Since this was to be strictly a reliability run, we had been cautioned not to let it turn into a race. We were sailing along at a good 25 miles an hour (which seemed swift-as-the-wind to us on this kind of road) when suddenly a huge Thomas Flyer roared by us, kicking up vast plumes of dust while the driver, Jack Mason, waved aloft a metal bottle as he steered the careening vehicle with one hand. His passengers were hanging on for dear life.

At first we were puzzled and a little annoyed at this careless manner of driving; but it soon became apparent *what* it was that Mason was waving. "Oh, he's not as crazy as he looks," I said. "He's the Goodyear man with the bottles of compressed air so we won't have to pump up tires." The Goodyear Company had offered to provide 16 of these for the convenience of the participating motorists—a very thoughtful and gracious piece of advertising!

Blue Point could not arrive too soon for me. My early breakfast was far in the past! Finally, after what seemed an interminable morning, we drew up in a shady grove where fires were giving off an enticing aroma. As we alighted rather stiffly, Mr. Kelsey and the passengers in the Maxwell automobiles, including Bob Clothier and Alfred Reeves, gathered around and there was a flurry of introductions. The steaks, however, proved a great lure and we became too engrossed in our repast to do more than note that Mr. Kelsey was talking in an undertone to Berry at one side, I overheard him say "…astounding skill…never saw anything like it…" but I went ahead with the job at hand and heard no more. Little did I realize that the conversation had been about me.

Several times during the meal of lobster, crabs and clams along with baked squash and "roasting ears" I found Mr. Kelsey staring at me, which was hard for me to understand. As engines were cranked Mr. Kelsey came toward us and said:

"Please take the lead this time, Mrs. Ramsey."

"If you wish," I replied—silently wondering why the request.

Just as we started we spied the little Ford runabout which Roy Chapin

19

had driven from Detroit. It was a saucy looking little thing with its bright brass band around the radiator. We liked it, in spite of our loyalty to the Maxwell.

The road narrowed considerably from here to Southampton, 30 miles away, and if one auto wished to pass another, one of them had to take to the dirt in doing so. Earl Ovington on his F-N motorcycle flew by, traveling fast in the opposite direction. He was courier for the officials of the run who realized the advantages of the two-wheeled vehicle on the narrow sections of the road.

"What's Mr. Ovington doing? He'll kill himself!"

I slowed momentarily at the top of a rise in the hills and saw Ovington pushing his machine up the embankment evidently intending to ride the ties. Berry suggested probably he couldn't make sufficient headway on the road. just then Ovington reached a small bridge over a stream, The cycle slipped to one side, pitching its rider down the bank with the machine in pursuit.

"Don't stop," said Berry. "A scout car has seen him and is going to help him. We'd only hold up all the rest."

Depressed by the episode I kept on. Rough surfaces made me fight the wheel continually. We stopped but a moment at Southampton and put out on the final lap. Suddenly we came to the dunes after a few miles of fairly good road, and just two sandy ruts lay ahead.

"Hang on!" I called to my passengers, an utterly needless warning as they were already clinging to the sides of the auto, wild-eyed.

The route now became a natural roller-coaster, a bit too scary to be much fun. First up sandy inclines, then down long slopes, we zoomed along on our way to the Point. The way appeared endless and the daylight was beginning to fade. It couldn't be *much* farther.

Suddenly Maggie exclaimed: "Looks like a light." It was the first word she had uttered since getting a death grip on the side of the Maxwell as we reached the dunes.

"That must be the lighthouse at the Point," added Nettie, with satisfaction and relief in her voice as an unmistakable beam traversed the sky, now nearly dark

Before we realized it, we mounted the last dune and there before us was the Montauk Inn. Many lights circled around as drivers sought places for the autos to remain overnight. We joined the others, were checked in by

20

the officials and climbed gratefully down from our seats. At the dock were other lights which glowed from the steamer *Shinnecock*, brought down from New York to accommodate the crowd, too large for the Inn to entertain.

A great thrill of surprise came over us as we found Ovington in the group. When we asked anxiously about his condition, he replied, "Oh I'm fine. Rode on in after they fished me from the ditch."

The first person we saw as we boarded the steamer was Mr. Kelsey. "Come on," he said, "I'm holding a table for the Maxwell party."

No wonder he had saved a table for us! He had something in mind for me—an across-the-continent safari of veil, duster and tire iron!

* * *

And now, as I stretched on my bed in Poughkeepsie, I thought of this whole adventure and Mr. Kelsey and wondered whether I should bless him or...

Notes

15. Alice's first car had a base price of $825 and a two-cylinder horizontally-opposed fourteen-horsepower engine. The car was introduced in 1908, three years after the Maxwell company was formed. The runabout was $25 cheaper than Ford's Model T, also introduced in 1908.
16. Hell Gate is in East River, not on the Atlantic Ocean. It separates Queens from the Bronx.
17. Montauk Point, on the eastern tip of Long Island, was the terminus of the race, and also of the fabulous career of Carl Graham Fisher. The Indianapolis multi-millionaire was head of the Prest-O-Lite company, suppliers of acetlyne gas for automobile headlights in the pre-electrical age. Fisher was the founder of the Lincoln Highway, the Dixie Highway, and developer of Miami Beach. When he tried to duplicate that success at Montauk Point, he was tripped up by the Great Depression and died penniless in 1937.
18. "Bone" was Alice's nickname for her husband, John Rathbone Ramsey. An attorney, he was Clerk of Bergen County in 1909. He was a Republican, elected to the U. S. Congress in 1917 from a heavily-Democratic Congressional district, he served two terms. He died in Hackensack in 1934 at age 74. Their home was at 221 Louis Street, now the home of the Women's Club of Hackensack.

19. Actually, Alice's mother-in-law, Martha Ramsey.
20. The Maxwell-Briscoe Company was flying high in 1909, but began a decline in 1920, when overproduction left their dealers with 20,000 unsold cars. Walter P. Chrysler rescued the firm, and the nameplate was discontinued in 1925, when he founded Chrysler Corporation, now Daimler-Chrysler. The popular name of the Maxwell DA was "Maxwell 30," because of its thirty-horsepower engine.
21. There is an ad in the 1908 *Blue Book* from the Warner Instrument Co., Beloit, Wisc., offering the Warner "Autometer," which measured both mileage and speed. Alice's car could have been equipped with this instrument.
22. Also the case with Ford's Model T, introduced in 1908, where the gas tank was beneath the front seat.
23. Pelham Manor is about forty miles east of Hackensack, near the west shore of Long Island Sound. Alice probably drove the little Runabout east on Hackensack's Essex Street, then through Bogata along the Fort Lee road. She would have boarded the ferry to cross the Hudson River near the site of present George Washington Bridge, then probably joined the ancient Boston Post Road to Pelham Manor. At least a three-hour adventure, one way. By the time she returned to Hackensack, this 21-year-old girl would have been completely captivated by the thrill of the open road, which stayed with her for the next seventy-four years of her life.
24. Columbus Circle is on Broadway, several blocks south of the Maxwell dealership.
25. The resulting gas was piped through rubber tubes to the headlamps, then lighted with a match. Carl Fisher's fortune came from his marketing tanks of compressed acetylene gas, thus eliminating the need for the pellets.

3

Poughkeepsie to Auburn, New York

DURING my years at Vassar, the principal hotel—almost the only place one could go for a real good dinner—was the dear old homey Nelson House.[26] When family or special friends arrived, it was a "party" to be taken there; and you may believe we Vassar girls looked forward to those occasions. So it was a pleasant spot in our recollections. This time was no disappointment, either. Welcomed as old friends, we were now regarded with extra distinction. The Maxwell was housed by Mr. Sague, the local agent, and returned to us in the morning ready for the day's jaunt, fueled, washed and once more lovely to behold.

After the restfulness of a good night's sleep, we set forth hopefully. It was still raining lightly and we continued with chains and rain togs. From here north we were not so familiar with the country and Nettie opened the *Blue Book* for directions to follow.

Blue Books were guides to certain sections of our states and were almost indispensable to motorists who ventured from home base. There were no *free* maps then, obtainable for the asking. The dependable *Blue Book* with its accurate mileages from one town to another and detailed instructions where to turn or which fork in the road to choose, was nearly as necessary as gasoline in the fuel tank. Preparation of these travel aids must have required a great deal of time, and publication was made very gradually. The first volume was New York State, followed by New England; one by one other sections were added. By 1909 they extended only to the Missouri River, leaving a vast void in the great wide West. But by 1920 they not only covered all the states but had a transcontinental issue known as Volume T. With the improvement of roads and placing of signposts, the need for them diminished and the once indispensable *Blue Book* became relegated to the shelf and assumed its new role as a museum piece. Then the oil companies took over and distributed good maps gratis to their customers.

Nettie had now located the correct route in the book and said, "What's this? 'Blue Stores'? Do you suppose *that* could be the name of an actual place?"

No one knew the answer to her inquiry. We'd heard a lot of funny names for towns and villages, but that seemed pretty much of a record. Sure enough, as we approached the little crossroads, there was a group of buildings, every one of them painted a bright, bright sky-blue. You just couldn't miss either the place or its color!

Poughkeepsie being the half-way point between New York and Albany, we could scarcely expect to get beyond the capital on the second day. At Albany we were to meet our advance agent, John D. Murphy, automobile editor of the *Boston Herald*. We had learned he had been engaged by the Company to follow along our route each day, usually by train, arrive at our destination ahead of us and obtain accommodations at a hotel. How would this work out, we wondered? We chatted about it as we drove north past the handsome estates of Frederick Vanderbilt at Hyde Park (a village not yet in the national limelight) and of John Jacob Astor near Rhinebeck.[27] We slipped and slid all through the morning, just missing the side supports of a small bridge, and continued with little in the way of diversion.

Tires of that epoch were built with a canvas foundation and the surface exposed to the road was entirely smooth (non-skid treads not having been introduced that early). They naturally offered no resistance to the slippery clay so, without the gripping of chains, it was an easy matter to slide off the highway into the ditch at the side.

Where modern automobiles use tires which measure perhaps 15x7 or 8 inches, the 1909 autos ran on wheels which utilized casings 32x4 inches. This greater wheel diameter raised the chassis higher above ground level

John D. Murphy of the Boston Herald, *our publicity man.*

and helped the transmission and differential escape possible damage from high centers between ruts made by wagon traffic.

Most manufacturers built autos conforming to the usual wagon tread, fifty-six inches in the North and sixty in the South. This caused great confusion for several years and it was both an uncomfortable and ludicrous situation for an auto with a fifty-six inch tread to travel ruts made by a sixty-inch tread vehicle. With one wheel down and the other on higher ground, the lop-sided ride was anything but delightful! Later, development of roads designed for motoring did away with those ridiculous differentiations and

fifty-six inches became the national standard. Half a century later the introduction of the small foreign motors and the new compacts has brought in
still narrower treads, but the roads are no problem now, unless one goes far
afield.

A few miles below Albany, when we could see the dome of the Empire State capitol, rising above the hill on which it stands, we veered to the
westward and finally crossed the bridge over the diminutive Hudson, not far
from its source, and entered the city.[28] At the Central Garage we found "J.D."
Murphy awaiting us, after his train trip from Boston.[29]

He was a good-looking neatly-groomed Irishman with curly hair.
Whatever fears we may have entertained before we met him were completely
erased during his weeks with us. He was always thoughtful and considerate
and gentlemanly; and we have only the best memories of his association and
helpfulness in every way.

Of course, we were rather ignorant concerning the duties and advantages of an advance agent, especially regarding an automobile journey. We
were acquainted with the fact that P. T. Barnum and circuses in general had
some such person going on ahead of the organization putting advance publicity in the newspapers and drumming up trade for the performances by
passing out free tickets and otherwise arranging for large crowds to attend.
But to be accompanied by a highly-galvanized gentleman speeding along
our route by train, attempting to reach our destination either ahead of us or at
the same time, was an experience to which we had to adjust. It was indeed a
novel form of amusement to watch the operations of such a man in our be-
half. It goes without saying that we would not have chosen this accompaniment, but the Maxwell firm insisted that the spectacle of four women driving
across country over practically uncharted wilderness was a golden opportunity for building up their own prestige in the automobile industry,

We admit that "J.D." was fully aware of the chance that had come to
him and that he made the most of it. And in the end we all had to say we were
glad he had come with us.

At a lunch counter we ordered some hot soup and during the meal
"J.D." asked many questions about our drive so far. He inquired in minute
detail and took copious notes, as if he were going to write an entire book on
our first day's happenings. We found it difficult to make monumental adventures out of occasional skids on wet clay roads, which seemed the chief oc-

cupation of the past 24 hours. But when it was time for us to depart on the afternoon drive, he appeared satisfied in respect to his information and the interview was concluded for the time being.

We were not too confident of adding a great number of miles to this day's run but set out from Albany westward knowing that every mile we could add was that much to the good on our way to Buffalo, where personal friends awaited our arrival.[30]

Well out into farm country we came upon two heavy wagons with teams blocking the road as the drivers conversed together. We began to speculate out loud whether they would be the type of intolerant farmer who resented the coming of the machine age and, to register their opposition, continue to occupy the road—or whether they would arrange for us to pass. Those men had a solution all their own—and simple it was. As we came near, the wagon going our way moved ahead slowly, circled around to the left and assumed the place originally held by the other. In similar fashion the other wheeled around behind us as we advanced and in a very easy way they had removed the obstruction and continued their conversation practically uninterrupted. When they finished talking all they had to do was complete the circle and go where they wished. We smiled at them in acknowledgment and giggled over the simple interchange.

The engine purred along sweetly and uncomplainingly as we pursued our route on the north side of the curving Mohawk. The rain was lessening. Like a coopful of little chickens which have been housed by a rainstorm, we began to peek out at the lovely rolling hills and beautiful scenery about us. It looked now as if it really might clear, but the condition of the road still obliged us to wear chains. We were anxious to remove them for the smooth-tread tires could not endure such treatment long without showing marked signs of wear. We had already replaced a couple of casings because of chain wear.

Finally we approached Amsterdam. Posters told us that a circus was in town. We were unanimous in the opinion that this was one of the most unattractive towns we had yet seen. No doubt we were prejudiced by our unfortunate introduction to the town, for the street was in a frightful state. Whatever kind of paving had originally surfaced the roadway was broken into ragged and jagged chunks, through which we had to thread our way gingerly to avoid damage to the car and tires, not to mention the discomfort to the occupants of the vehicle.

But even this dismal prospect turned out to have a silver lining. All this jouncing, in addition to the hours of elapsed time, had sharpened our outlook for signs of available food. And right here we spied a tiny, inconspicuous restaurant. Just why we should have been drawn to the particular spot is a poser, for it was just a little place frequented by trolley men at the terminus of their line. The magnet which attracted us inescapably proved to be some homemade vegetable soup, which the waitress served with a plate of bread. It all sounds—and looked—prosaic enough, but oh, *what* vegetable soup! Seasoned perfectly, with loads of meat and vegetables, it was like the nectar of the gods to us. And a meal in itself! Giving ourselves a pat on the back for having happened so luckily on the find, we went out cheered and well satisfied.

Proceeding into Amsterdam, we saw that the hour was already four-thirty. Though we had covered but slightly over a hundred miles that day—getting a new tire in place of a worn one, meeting and talking with "J.D." at Albany, and stopping many times to attach the dangling ends of rattling chains—it seemed to me it might be well to stop right here for the night. So I said, "What do you say to staying here at the Hotel Warner and getting off early tomorrow? It's too far to Utica for the night, and the towns between are pretty small. Let's call it a day."[31]

Everyone accepted the suggestion and we eagerly sought our rooms to clean up and catch a little rest before dinner. "J.D." arrived later by train. I never could figure out how he knew in what town he would find us!

In the morning the muddy roads continued as far as Little Falls, when skies finally broke clear and we were able to remove those horrible (though valuable) chains. Cross-pieces had been replaced in them as they wore and broke apart but they still had played the same noisy tune.[32]

As we stopped for lunch at the Hotel Martin in Utica, we were more than surprised to have the accompaniment of music.[33] This was truly a metropolitan atmosphere of sophistication which contributed a note of gaiety to our meal. The head waiter and his staff were most solicitous for our comfort. We would have liked to remain and enjoy this diversion to the full, but we put out for Syracuse. As we entered this city, another welcoming party of several autos took us to the Bristol and Daly agency and insisted on being our hosts at The Hub. We didn't *need* food that soon! When it turned out to be our evening meal, however—because we did not arrive at Auburn until seven-forty—we were glad we had accepted their gracious hospitality.[34]

Driving up before the Osborne House, we saw "J.D." pacing up and down the sidewalk. The first words he uttered were, "Where on earth have you been? Gee, I was worried!"

By the time we had explained we had been held up an extra half-hour by a Franklin stuck in the mud just outside Auburn, "J.D." had had time to restore his equilibrium and was once more his jolly self. He really had quite a job keeping track of four wandering females!

Notes

26. Nelson House was on the Albany Post road, also Market Street, between Main and Cannon Streets. Nothing remains but a much later addition.
27. Franklin D. Roosevelt was five years older than Alice in 1909, but not living at Hyde Park at the time she motored by. He was beginning his career with a prominent law firm at New York City.
28. Alice took the Old Greenbush Bridge across the Hudson, entering the city on South Ferry Street. It was replaced in 1933 by the old Dunn Memorial Bridge, still later by the present bridge of the same name.
29. Albany garages were unimpressive to the compilers of the 1908 and 1910 city directories, and the Central Garage does not show up in either. The capital of New York State, Albany's population was 100,253 in the 1910 census.
30. Alice's route here cannot be determined from this narrative. She probably proceeded west from Albany on Central Street (NY 5), to cross the Mohawk near Schenectady.
31. Amsterdam's Hotel Warner boasted a café, grill, pool room, and barbershop. Later named the Amsterdam Hotel, it was at 101 East Main Street, next door to the Opera House. Alice would have entered the city on East Main, now also Route 5, but Route 5 turns south as Front Street, along the north bank of the Mohawk. A shopping mall occupies the hotel site today.
32. The chains wreaked havoc on the old tread-less tires. They were needed between the towns, for most of the roads were not hard surfaced in1909. But the roads in the towns and cities were mostly macadam or other hard surfaces, which tended to wear out both chains and tires. The most popular brand was Weed Chains. There was a Weed ad in the 1908 *Blue Book*.
33. Hotel Martin, built late in the nineteenth century, was razed in 1966. Alice has been on NY 5 all the way from Auburn. She turned south to cross the Mohawk

(and the Erie Canal) to enter Utica, a city of 74,000 people.
34. The Hub is long gone. It was at 124-126 West Washington Street. Alice was still driving on NY 5, which is Erie Blvd. in Syracuse. The city had a population of 137,249 in 1910. Auburn's leading hotel, the huge Osborne House, was erected in 1904, and was gone by 1918.

4

Auburn to Chicago, Illinois

WE ALL agreed we never wanted to see "Copper John" again. "Copper John" was the huge figure of a soldier cast in metal on top of the Auburn State Prison.

Upon our arrival in town, we learned of an invitation from Warden Benham, head of the institution, to inspect his domain with *him* as our personal escort. This was a very special favor, as we truly recognized. Somewhat dubious of the delights of visiting a state prison, in spite of the realization of the implied attention, I wondered how the girls would react to the project.

"Well," said Nettie, who usually took the lead and showed her position, "I can't say that is my greatest desire. But I'm sure the offer is a special courtesy and I don't see how we can turn it down." I had felt the same way, but waited for their expression before saying anything definite. Maggie, as usual, echoed Nettie's view. Hermine, on the contrary, showed real interest and curiosity. Good girl! She was out to see things on this trip and she enjoyed everything.

"Anyhow," continued Nettie, "let's go as early as we can, so we are not too late getting on our way."

It was unanimously agreed that was an excellent idea, so we went over immediately after breakfast. The warden was most kind in giving us so much of his personal attention, and the inspection was educational and interesting—though scarcely pleasant. The stone gang was sitting near the wall of a building, each man with a hammer, breaking big stones into little ones, under the surveillance of a watchful guard. It occurred to us—if tedium alone can punish, these inmates must indeed have suffered. Even so, perhaps *they* were better off than the men confined to their tiny cells, divorced from association and conversation with their fellow beings. We could well understand now why they all looked forward to being able to gaze upon the figure of "Copper John" once more. It could *only* be seen from points *outside* the prison wall.

In spite of our education on penal institutions, we were greatly relieved to complete the tour and return to the Maxwell in the outer yard where *we* could wave goodbye to the copper statue.

Bidding farewell to Warden Benham, we started toward the automobile. I gave the crank an unusually vigorous twirl. Nothing happened! Again and again! Still no response! Raising the hood and looking over spark plugs and wiring still brought no results and I suspected by now something vital was at fault. The man from the garage worked for an hour with no more success. Reluctant to waste any more time, we telephoned back to Bristol and Daly at Syracuse for expert help. Meanwhile the Maxwell was towed back to the hotel yard to await the arrival of the repair man. Here, passing residents gathered with curiosity to see what ailed the motorized contraption. One youngster, with mocking scorn, yelled "Get a horse!," the familiar form of derision. In reply I said, defensively: "That's just what I tried to do, Sonny."

As a matter of fact it was a horse named Duke that was actually responsible for getting me into this predicament.

Duke was my husband's bay horse and, even though we had been married over two years, I had never driven Duke alone. He was stabled with the handsome family team a few doors away from our home, where Mother Ramsey and Bone's two sisters were living. York, the colored coachman, cared for the horses, and his wife Laura was the family cook. They had been with the Ramseys for many years.

I had always been fond of horses and hoped I would some day have one of my own. Today I had the urge to drive Duke, so I plucked up courage and broached the subject hopefully.

"Bone," I said, "do you think I might take Duke for a short drive today?"

We were at breakfast and the colored maid was bringing in the customary meat and potatoes. To a conservative husband that wasn't just the moment for a possible family debate. So he threw in my direction a slightly amused smile and, with a twinkle in his eye, waited for her exit.

Then the subject was opened again.

"Where did you think of going?" he asked.

"Oh, just for a little ride in town," I replied.

"Duke has a pretty tough mouth, you know. Do you think you can manage him?"

"Yes, I think I can. My arms are strong."

"Well, all right," said Bone. "I'll tell York to harness him to the runabout and bring him to the door. But be careful."

I assured him I would, happy with anticipation.

There was a chill in the air but the balminess of promised spring was on its way and in the early afternoon the colored coachman appeared at the front door with Duke and the rubber-tired carriage.

As I took my seat in the open vehicle, Duke turned his head around and gave me a glassy stare. York and my husband were his sole drivers. Could he perhaps be trying to convince me that he wasn't going to permit a "mere female" to tell *him* what to do or where to go? Not if I knew it! So, picking up the reins, which I noted (partly with a feeling of nervousness but also with a conviction of security) had large loops on them for extra pulling grip, I started down the street with Duke at a walk, gradually increasing into a demure-enough trot.

Pride welled up within me and a great sense of satisfaction. At last I was having the pleasure of driving a horse and rig "on my own."

There was a plan in my mind to drive around a large block of streets which would take me westward on Central Avenue across the railroad and trolley tracks, past the High School (which I had attended a few years before) and up the hill to the pretty residential district on Prospect Avenue; then on to Passaic Street, again turning right, descending the hill and so home.

Suddenly behind us, I heard an approaching automobile. This was the spring of 1908 and there were probably not half a dozen motor vehicles in Hackensack. People were as yet completely unaccustomed to horseless carriages and, naturally, horses couldn't see anything good about them. For so many decades *they* had been King of the Highways and they resented with fierce intensity the approach of a truly horseless carriage. Many jokes were told about taking automobiles apart and hiding the pieces in the bushes until the frightened animal had passed. Why—oh why, did one have to come along at this particular time?

Duke began laying back his ears as the sound of the motor came nearer. I wasn't exactly scared, but I realized I better be prepared for some sort of crisis. *And it happened!* Just as the monster overtook us there was a loud *Honk! Honk!* and George Johnson in his new Pierce-Arrow runabout flew by at a 30-mile clip.[35]

That was all Duke needed to display what *his* speed was! He gave one snort, and put out for parts unknown. I found suddenly what those loops on the reins were for!—and rejoiced in their presence. Bracing my feet against the sloping portion of the floor I grabbed the forward loops and pulled with all my might, gently coaxing him with "Whoa, Duke, whoa," as we flew up the empty street. Duke's feet pounded on the solid macadam road like a group of trip hammers. No one was in sight except the driver of that tooting automobile and he was now well up the hill on his way to the Golf Club.

Happily, that hill was dead ahead and as I pulled hard on the bit and Duke made his way up the grade, he *had* to slow down. I spoke to him gently as we went along and soon he was calmed down once more and we proceeded sedately enough back to the stable.

That evening I related the story to Bone. He first looked a little frightened and asked if I was all right. Oh yes, I was. However, when the suggestion of a horse of my own was made, Bone had a new idea and said, "Why get a horse at all? The man from the Maxwell agency thinks you could drive an automobile without any trouble. How would you like to have one of those instead of a horse?"

It wasn't exactly the same as a live animal with which one could have a certain sense of companionship. But I took to mechanics rather naturally, and the thought of getting places was most alluring. There *were* drawbacks to tending live animals which an inanimate auto would not have. So the vote was cast in favor of an automobile; and a small garage to house it was erected at the rear of our property.

* * *

The repair man from Bristol and Daly now arrived and fortunately brought with him a new coil, which proved to be the seat of our difficulty. By five-thirty in the afternoon we were finally in a condition to proceed and set out for Buffalo, 138 miles away. This was a greater distance than we had covered in any previous *full* day's time, but the roads were now dry and the weather clear, and there were no chains to hamper our progress. We sped along at a good clip. The country was beautiful in its fresh cleanliness after the rain and we all felt made over.[36]

Eventually dusk came on and, with it, light-up time. The brass headlamps had been protected during the rain, when they were not in use, by

On our way to Buffalo we prepare to light acetylene lamps. Note the windshield rolled up at front end of car top.

pantasote "raincoats." These the girls now removed while I started the routine of illumination. The preliminaries completed, I got out those blessed wind matches which would keep burning in any gale until they burned themselves out. Presto! Now we can find our way for hours across the Empire State to Buffalo—we hope!

After dark, objects took on an entirely different aspect in the eerie artificial light. We resumed a fair speed; but Maggie seemed to be suffering from a case of the jitters. Every little thing along the roadside was another spook to her. First the shining eyes of a cat gave her a scare; then a particularly menacing apparition, looking for all the world like a brilliantly illuminated trolley car on the left, turned out to be nothing more than a group of milk cans waiting to be picked up for the creamery. Several rabbits enlivened the evening on their way to a juicy garden patch while the farmer wasn't looking. These various ghostlike apparitions increased the tension of the lonely drive. On and on we went. There were few on the road but us and the time ticked by until at last we drove up at the entrance to the Iroquois Hotel. It was one-fifteen in the morning and we scrambled into bed, tired, triumphant, but with less order than speed, to sleep well—and late.[37]

Next morning I put in a telephone call to my friends, only to find, to my consternation that several of them had driven to *Rochester* and were still there, awaiting our arrival!!!! We'd never even thought of going to Rochester—it was off the direct route. We were sorely disappointed after making such a strenuous effort to reach Buffalo before Sunday. They hurried back, however, to have dinner with us.[38]

Out came the one dressy suit that each of us carried in her suitcase, and to my utter amazement my three companions produced beflowered and beribboned hats of ample dimension. Where they hid them I'll never know: I had to be content with my one motoring cap with stiff visor and full blousy crown. In the front, like a Cyclops with his single eye in the center of his forehead, was one piece of decoration—the bronze medal I had received at the end of the Montauk Point Run.

Thus decked out, we were ready for a round of sightseeing with our friends, beginning with dinner at the Park Club. The following day a drive along The Front, beside the swift current of the Niagara River, culminated at magnificent Niagara Falls.[39]

But good and happy days cannot continue forever with an expedition on the agenda, so with an extra play day behind us, we set out for the Middle West.

Southward near the shore of Lake Erie the route led past some of the most lovely vineyards of western New York State, whose wines and grape juice are well-known. With roads and weather favorable, we found our drive this day a delightful one, In Erie we saw the handsome new building of the Elks' organization; and one of my college friends and her companion escorted us out of town—only to have *their* car break down. They insisted that we proceed and we waved a reluctant but sympathetic farewell and went on toward Cleveland.[40]

We followed the *Blue Book* directions from town to town and found them helpful until we came to one which read: "At 11.6 miles, yellow house and barn on rt. Turn left."

Arrived at this point, we looked in vain for a yellow house.

"I don't see any yellow house. Do you?" I inquired.

They agreed as one. I thought I had watched the odometer reading carefully, but there was a chance I had misread it or had not remembered correctly. So I decided to go on to the next corner.

We found a woman working in the front yard of a house which was not yellow, either. I called out to her, "Will you please tell me if that road goes to Cleveland?"

"Oh no," said the woman with a peculiar little smile, "that road is a mile back."

"By the green house?" I asked.

"That's right."

"But the *Blue Book* says to 'turn by a yellow house," I called back to her.[41]

"Yes, I know," she said, laughing, "there's been a lot of trouble about that. You see, last year the man wanted to paint his house and barn, and he decided to change the color. He's 'agin' auto*mo*biles. So he said, 'Now you watch! We'll have some fun with them auto*mo*bile drivers.' He'll be all right when he gets one himself," she said, with another chuckle.

Enjoying the humor, and being set on the right path, we retraced the mile and made the turn toward Cleveland. From that time on we were always a trifle suspicious of directions which depended on the color of a building! You couldn't dispute the *right* of a man to change the color of his own dwelling, but it didn't make for accuracy in traveling the right route.

At Willoughby, twenty miles east of Cleveland, Mr. Bleasdale, Mr. Charles Carpenter and a group of reporters eagerly awaited our arrival. How long had they been there? There was no definite way for them to know our arrival time, especially when we were shown so much attention enroute. But we were gratefully relieved of the anxiety of finding our way through the city. We twisted and wriggled through town, viewing some of the sights on the way.[42]

Greeters in Ohio.

An interesting innovation in Cleveland was the brick street paving on Euclid Avenue. In the east we were accustomed to the use of brick in the building of houses, but we had never before seen it used for road surface.[43]

We turned a corner and heard a strange horn.

38

"Whatever can that be?" said Hermine.

"Sounds like a hunting horn," Maggie replied.

"The middle of a city is a funny place for that sort of thing," remarked Nettie.

I was just listening hard, trying to locate the source of the sound. Just then a handsome car joined the little parade which was forming. The driver was holding his hand at the side of the vehicle playing four keys which evidently activated the bugle-like notes. This was a resonantly pleasant device for warning a pedestrian to get out of the way! The driver, Mr. Claude Foster, saw our approving expressions, and when we arrived at the Hollenden Hotel offered to present us with one for the Maxwell and install it in the morning. This seemed like a very pretty way of announcing our arrival at the entrance of towns on the route and we agreed to drive over to the factory after breakfast the next day. The horn was a special product of Cleveland, manufactured by the Gabriel Company which also made the early type of shock absorber known as the Gabriel Snubber. Mr. Foster was the head of this company.

The installing of the horn occupied the entire morning so that we were unable to leave for Toledo until after lunch. It also furnished the one occasion when Nettie voiced disapproval of our action. Perhaps she didn't mean it as such; but I am sensitive, and I was anxious that they should enjoy the trip as much as possible. We had all been quite encouraged by the 198-mile drive from Buffalo to Cleveland. When the following day added but 132, Nettie, with small but recognizable suspicion of complaint in the tone of her voice remarked, "Well, if we hadn't spent the whole morning having that horn put on, we could have made more." I was a trifle hurt, for *I* was responsible for it. It was her first and last criticism, however, so I forgot it. The next day, one of the wires which operated the horn snapped and it was temporarily out of commission.

Setting out for Toledo, piloted again by Mr. Carpenter with Mr. James Couzens, Mr. Forbes and Mr. Craig, we were seemingly in for a hoodoo day. First came the incident of the horn, then the pilot car had a puncture. We waited to see if we could render assistance but they urged us to go on; so with thanks for their company this far, we bade adieu. After a short stop at a lunch counter in Lorain, *we* had a blowout, then got stuck in a bad piece of road before entering Toledo. We had been able to work up the terrific speed of 42 miles per hour on the Cleveland Parkway—our record so far. That helped to make up for some of the other delays. Forty miles east of Toledo we were met by Mr. Davis of Detroit, Mr. Moran and a reporter, Mr. Smith.[44] Another rainy day as we prepared to leave Toledo. Mr. Moran led the way and "J.D." rode with him, By now our advance agent must have found it difficult to tell where our day's travel would end. We would plan to reach Chicago, but never knew where night would find us. Mileage had improved considerably over our first few days, however, with 132, 151, and again 132, which we thought very good. The roads were not so excellent as we had anticipated—very bumpy and rough. Chubby "J.D." looked awfully funny bouncing around like a baby in the other auto. Mr. Moran accepted the punishment to his car and himself as far as Wauseon, where he was our host at luncheon, and on to Ligonier; then *he* took the road to Fort Wayne.[45] We kept on to Goshen, with "J.D." squeezed in with us.

Our gentleman courier here took the train to Chicago and we agreed to meet him at the Auditorium Annex the next day. We were pleasantly surprised to find fine roads with a limestone foundation. These, when dry, gave off great quantities of white dust which, under the heavy traffic of autos returning from that day's running of the Cobe Cup automobile races, well-nigh choked us. Added to that some reckless and inconsiderate driving on the part of people who wanted to reach home ahead of everyone else, and it was a rather unpleasant approach to Chicago.

One Cadillac, pulling around to pass us on the right struck and dented our hub cap and, in the fray, lost his entirely; but he never stopped. Our first experience with a hit-and-run driver.

Across northern Indiana there was an unexpected change in the landscape in the form of numerous hillocks of varying heights. They seemed somehow very strange and misplaced in this flattish area. Finally we found a few that were quite bare of any vegetation and were surprised to discover they were sand dunes! Sand dunes in the middle of our country that far from the sea? Ah yes, but *these* had been built from sand blown up by the strong winds off the Great Lakes—a thing which had never before occurred to us as a possibility.[46]

Another surprise awaited us as we neared the Windy City. Back in grade school we had learned that Chicago was a large railroad center. We believed it, all right, but that day we had a practical application of the fact which would make the knowledge stick in our minds forever. For miles and miles we crossed tracks—singly, in pairs, and in groups; back and forth we wound around and over them until we almost got dizzy and wondered if there would ever be an end. Bump! Bump! up and down, again and again. Springs were sturdy or they never would have endured such jouncing. They were far from the rocking chair variety, however!

More than twenty years had passed since Mrs. O'Leary's cow had kicked over the lantern and caused the Great Fire. Chicago was beginning to show signs of becoming the metropolis it now is, with all the splendid new buildings. Michigan Avenue was already asphalt-paved and a beautiful wide thoroughfare lined with bustling offices and stores.[47]

Almost the first greeting from "J.D." was, "Mr. Handley, head of the Maxwell factory at Newcastle, has invited you four ladies and me to be his guests at the Cobe Cup Race at Crown Point tomorrow."[48]

We were most impressed and asked questions. Yes, it would be necessary to leave *very* early as it was 47 miles to the track and we must get into our parking places in good time. We were game! We rose at three in the morning—I can't say "bright and early." It was plenty *early*—but not yet *bright!*

There was a continuous caravan of automobiles—apparently all going to the same spot. Hats, veils and dusters failed to keep us protected or clean, and by the time we arrived, people were calling out to us "Oh, you kid!" and "Why don't you wash your dirty faces?" We were truly sights! Where our goggles fitted around our eyes, excluding the dust, there were circular patches of skin several shades lighter than the rest of the face. We looked as if we belonged to another *race!* (No pun intended!)

The Cobe Cup races were the first *stock car* events of the kind to be held in the United States. Louis Chevrolet, whom I had met at the Daytona Beach (Florida) races in 1906, won in a Buick over Bourque in a Knox and Robertson in a Locomobile. It was a great sports event; but a blisteringly hot sun, in which we sat for long hours, made us happy to achieve the shelter of our rooms where we could indulge in a hot bath.

This day's dissipation set us back on our sleeping hours so that we used Sunday as a real day of rest. Mr. Handley and his staff were fine hosts and did everything they could for our enjoyment, driving us through the city parks and even taking us out into the suburbs, where we dined with a Rathbone cousin of the Ramseys. Hermine took this occasion to be with her brother and a friend.

The following day we prepared the auto for its westward trek and figured our routes to Iowa. We lunched with friends, shopped, and even had the rejuvenation of a dry shampoo, Why "dry," my diary doesn't seem to say, but it does record that "it felt fine." We direly needed it and I'm sure it *must* have improved our appearance.

Of course, we had donned our city duds as soon as we reached Chicago. The change from wearing our traveling suits allowed the opportunity for a sweeping renovation of our wardrobes at the hands of the cleaners and the hotel laundry. Once more we were spotless from tip to toe. Glorious sensation!

Fourteen days now had elapsed since we departed from New York, though not all of them were spent on the road. We were but one-third of the distance across the continent, nevertheless. We filled up the Maxwell, went back to the covert cloth traveling suits—long skirts, tunic coats and all—pulled in our belts, girded ourselves for the coming fray, and sallied forth for whtever lay before us!

"City clothes" in Chicago.

Notes

35. The massive Pierce was one of the most prestigious cars in the world.
36. Alice was driving on what is now US 20. Just west of Avon she would have left that route to continue west on NY 5 to Buffalo.
37. The Iroquois was Buffalo's leading hotel in 1909. Following NY 5, Alice entered the city on Main Street and drove right to the Iroquois, in the heart of downtown. With a population of 423,715 in 1910, Buffalo was the tenth largest city in the United States.
38. Rochester is about eighty miles northeast of Buffalo.
39. As Alice rode north along the Niagara River, she would have noticed what seemed to be a low cloud up ahead. Actually, this is mist, rising from the falls. Just two months prior to her arrival, the American Falls were dry, blocked by an ice jam.
40. NY 5 often comes within yards of the shore of Lake Erie. Alice followed that highway along the lakeshore, through Erie, Pennsylvania, and into Ohio. Highway 5 would have joined present US 20 just east of the Ohio border.
41. Alice was driving near the Pennsylvania/Ohio border. Curiously, the 1908 *Blue Book* has no mention of such a spot in this area.
42. In 1909, Willoughby would have been a small town on the shore of Lake Erie. Today there is very little undeveloped land between Willoughby and Cleveland. Alice probably drove on Euclid Avenue from Willoughby west to Cleveland.
43. Cleveland in 1909 was the sixth largest city in America, with a population of 560,000. Alice would have joined present US 6 near the center of the city. She and her friends evidently stayed at the Hollenden Hotel, on US 6 (Superior Avenue) in downtown Cleveland. Built in 1885 at 600 E. Superior, it was demolished in 1963. The site is now Fifth Third Center Bank.
44. Toledo boasted a population of 168,000 in 1909. Alice probably crossed the Maumee River on Main Street and stopped at the Boody House to spend the night. Boody House, at 405 Madison Street, Toledo, was razed in 1929-30. The site is occupied today by National City Bank.
45. Alice's route to Ligonier, Indiana, is anybody's guess. She probably left Toledo on what became Ohio Route 2, later designated US 20A, paralleling I-80, which is a few miles to the north. Wauseon is on SR 2, so she probably stairstepped on 2 to Bryan, turning south there to hit the route of US 6. She probably followed US 6 into Indiana. The old road is about a mile north of present US 6 east of Ligonier—that's where Alice would have hit the route of the Lincoln Highway, still four years in the future, and she would follow it from here west to the Pacific Ocean in San Francisco. They spent the night in Goshen, probably at Hotel Hascall, on the north side of the courthouse.

46. Alice was driving the route of the future Lincoln Highway through northern Indiana, passing Elkhart, Osceola, Mishawaka, South Bend, New Carlisle, La Porte, Westville, and Valparaiso. There she left that route to pass through Hammond and entered Illinois at South Chicago. Along the way she passed the next to the dunes on the south shore of Lake Michigan, now designated as Indiana Dunes National Lakeshore.
47. The *Blue Book* route into the Windy City was a stairstep up to Michigan Avenue, which would have been followed all the way to the Loop.
48. Alice attended the first Cobe Cup Race held in Crown Point, Indiana, about six miles southwest of Merrillville and some forty-five miles southeast of Chicago's Loop. Held on June 19, the route covered twenty-three miles of dirt roads circling south and west of the Crown Point courthouse. The race was won by Louis Chevrolet, driving a 40-hp Buick. The race was named for Ira M. Cobe, head of the Chicago Automobile Club. That was part of the national American Automobile Association, founded in 1908. Cobe was one of the directors.

5

Chicago to the Mississippi River

SO FAR, you may feel as if the trip was a pretty tame procedure. Well, in the light of later travel—it was! just the same the weather of those first few days had made driving more precarious than most of my first year's experience (excluding the dunes drive on the Montauk Point Run).

People who were familiar with northern Illinois had advised our following a route through Geneva, DeKalb, Rochelle, Dixon and Fulton where we would cross the Mississippi River bridge to Clinton, Iowa, and on to Cedar Rapids. We fully hoped to reach the latter place that first day out of Chicago. There would be three autos for this portion of the way, as Mr. Handley, Mr. Creek and Mr. Spooner, the photographer, were to go part of the distance, and Mr. Milks of the Chicago agency would take "J.D." with him as far as Clinton. The third automobile contained Mr. Valentine of Rochelle. "J.D." could squeeze into our Maxwell from Clinton to Cedar Rapids.

As we departed from the Windy City we trustfully hoped for fair weather to continue. A crowd gathered along Michigan Avenue near the Maxwell showroom to watch us leave.[49] Our auto had now acquired slightly more equipment in the way of a stout towing rope, a block and tackle, and a short shovel. The bystanders appeared fascinated by the sturdy look of the vehicle so outfitted. In that section of the city the Western Union telegraph

What a stir for Michigan Avenue! The driver takes a backward glance.

service was temporarily at a standstill. Not a strike—not in those days. Just the delivery boy standing by the curb, dumbfounded—completely absorbed in the momentous departure of this automobile containing but four women! It was fairly early in the day so without doubt he must have had a batch of messages in his pocket to deliver. But—shucks!—they'd just *have* to wait. Who could expect him to miss this uncommon event?

Everyone waved and wished us good luck as we started.[50]

The section of Illinois westward from Chicago to the Mississippi is beautiful agricultural country of rich, black, fertile soil. The road was frequently crossed by small creeks making their way to the Rock River tributary of the Father of Waters.

Maggie spied one of the Shetland pony farms and exclaimed, "Oh,

46

Only one *looks apprehensive! It can't be the traffic—even in Chicago—in 1909!*

look at those cute ponies!"

Nettie's real love happened to be thoroughbred racing, so ponies didn't call forth any enthusiasm from her. Before long, however, as we drove on, I heard her say, "There, that's what I like to see. That's a breeding farm and they have some classy-looking youngsters in that field!"

My companions enjoyed this new feature in the landscape as we passed farm after farm, some with huge corn fields extending for great distances. On my part, I sneaked little side glances, too, but couldn't feast my eyes as they did. Other farms had dairy cattle—there was very little beef raised in this state as yet.

A sudden recollection came to my mind, called up by the sight of the cattle, and I proposed, "Nettie, tell Hermine the story of Whizzle's cow." I

Spooner & Wells Photo

You can see for yourself Western Union is at a standstill this morning.

put it that way so as not to give away the point.

Nettie responded with a chuckle and answered, "Oh surely. You remember Maggie's husband, don't you, Hermine? His right name is William but everyone calls him 'Whizzle.'"

"I think so," said Hermine, "the little dark man with the moustache."

"That's the one. Well, we used to drive out into the country in the carriage after Maggie and he were married, and of course we saw plenty of cows. We would point out different ones to him and tell him what breed they were. You see, he was raised in the city and didn't know much about such things. We had a lot of fun with him, telling him one was a buttermilk cow! We kept up that deception for a long time before he found out the truth and that we had been joshing him all that time!"

Hermine liked that tale, for she had been brought up in the dairy state of Wisconsin before becoming a resident of Hackensack.

We were just sobering up from our laugh over this when we noticed that Mr. Valentine had stopped his Maxwell and was making adjustments to his carburetor. As we slowed behind him, I felt a very suspicious bumping. Maggie, always alert for trouble, had noted it too and said, rather nervously:

"Something sounds funny. Is everything all right?"

"I suspect we have a flat," I groaned.

"Oh dear," Maggie remarked. "But it's nice the men are here to help."

"I can't let them do that. I'm supposed to do things like that myself," was my reply.

Of course the men offered, but I explained the way I felt about it.

We had our share of "flats." This photo shows arrangement of luggage and cover on rear lamp (oil) when not in use.

I hated to pump a tire. With all those able-bodied men standing around I would hate to *waste* their strength while I broke my back unnecessarily! So with a sly amused smile I resumed: "But this isn't an *exclusive* party. You may watch, if you like. And I *might* let you pump...'" We had a tank of compressed air for supplying air to the tires in emergency, but we all agreed it should be saved for flats on the desert or in the rain.

While this conversation was in progress, I had removed my coat and, crawling far enough under the cases at the rear, had placed the jack under the axle and raised the left rear tire off the ground. The men stood around feeling a little foolish and inept, no doubt, but respected my point of view on the matter. Maybe they were even a little curious, too.

I marshaled my group of willing helpers and tried to assume an executive attitude.

"Now, what can we do to help?" asked Maggie. "There *must* be something."

"All right," I said. "Nettie, would you please bring me the pliers and two tire irons from the tool box on the running board? They are pieces of steel about ten or twelve inches long. And, Hermine, there's a cylindrical box in the tire drum that says 'Tire Repair Kit.' I'll need that. Maggie, you might get out the pump. The men are going to need *that*," I finished, smiling.

This was all routine to me, except the novelty of a male audience. They stood near and looked on while I worked.

"What do you have to do?" asked Hermine.

"Well, first I raise the wheel off the ground, as you see; then with the pliers I loosen the circular nut at the base of the tire valve stem and remove the tire 'valve inside.' This requires a special little gem of a tool that I always carry in my pocket for safekeeping." With this remark I reached into said pocket and withdrew the "little darling." It was *that*, to me, as it was well-nigh impossible to take out a valve inside without it. "Now I have to pry off the outside bead of the casing in order to get the tube out."

Fortunately our Maxwell had advanced one step beyond the early clincher type of tire and rim which took a Samson to handle, especially if the tire had been in use for some time. Our rims were the quick-detachable type (known to the trade as Q-D's) and consisted of two metal rings—one a complete circle, the other a broken circle, one end of which was crooked for about one-half inch into a right angle shape. The projection so formed fitted into a hole in the rim on which the tire was mounted, so the rings did not slip their position. When the inner tube was inflated, the pressure kept the bead of the tire tightly wedged by the retaining rings.

Meanwhile I had inserted the tire irons and worked around the edge, forcing the bead over the rim—careful not to pinch the tube in so doing. After the near side was loosened, it was necessary to reach inside the casing and draw out the tube, as Mother used to extract the entrails of a turkey preparatory to stuffing it for Thanksgiving dinner!

"When you have it out, what do you do with it?" pursued Hermine.

"You either put in a fresh one or you repair this one on the spot. It will take a little longer to fix it but, in that way, we can keep our good tubes until we need them worse," sotto voce "when we're alone!"

It didn't take very long to find the pinch that caused the flat. Someone had inserted that tube carelessly.[51]

Nettie quickly remarked: "I'll bet *you* didn't mount that tire. You're too careful to pinch a tube." Confidence like that was music to my ears.

"Now, Hermine," I went on with my executive business, "open up the tire repair kit. Careful, don't drop anything. Please hand me the small file for roughing the rubber." She found that all right and after a few strokes, I applied the cement to that spot and to the under side of the patch to be applied to the pinch. These had to stand a few minutes until the cement became "tacky"; then I put them together, pressing firmly around the edges and holding them until they were set. Before replacing the tube in the casing, I felt carefully all around the inside of the tire to make sure there was no nail or other object which might give us more trouble. Then, dusting it within with talc and placing the tube with caution inside the "shoe" with the valve stem in place, and free, I replaced both rings and said: "Now, boys, it's ready for the pump. And—let's not be selfish about it—since there are several of you, you might take turns."

They manned the pump lustily and in no time we were ready to go. While they put forth their strength, we put away the other tools.

Mr. Valentine was pleased with his carburetor adjustment.

The girls had learned something about changing a tire.

And the Maxwell once more was happy to have four "feet"!

The road surface through this portion of Illinois was fairly good gravel base so we were not troubled with heavy going or bad ruts and we made quite good time—when we were in motion! Towns were not too far apart and each had a flavor of its own. DeKalb had a large post office, rather an impressive-looking building with a handsome copper dome which must have been the height of expensive architecture in those days.[52] The streets were lined with elms which made us think of the east and especially New England. No doubt some former resident of that part of our country had located here and planted elms, reminiscent of home.

Now we saw plenty of pigs, for a change: big pigs, little pigs, all sizes and all different colors, and all over the roads as well as the fields. We hadn't realized there were so many different kinds. Pigs to us were just pigs. But we always uttered a little squeal of pleasure whenever we saw them scampering along. They seemed to tickle our risibles.

We learned one bit of historical interest when they told us that Joseph F. Glidden (not the one of the Glidden Tours) lived in DeKalb and had been the inventor of barbed wire—that diabolical instrument of Lucifer if you caught your skirt or trousers on it, yet what a boon to the farmer who wanted to keep his cattle in and outsiders out. It was invented in 1873 and then was manufactured in DeKalb for many years thereafter.[53]

The terrain was now slightly more rolling than in the eastern part of the state and the pleasant pastoral landscape would hold great allurement to any painter who beheld it. The horses with low arched necks, drinking from the little streams, were a beautiful picture of homey contentment.

The Maxwell and its occupants were contented, too, as they made their way westward.

Our entry into Rochelle, Illinois, had been delayed for so long that we found the dining room of the hotel closed for noon dinner and were obliged to patronize a small restaurant. The meal was evidently not too gratifying as my diary says: "The men filled up on buttermilk and we all had bread and butter and sugar as side dishes." That meant that good food was scarce![54]

Food in general across the country was fair—sometimes poor. Whenever it became too sketchy, we could always get along by eating a slice or two of bread with the addition of butter and sugar for nourishment and energy. Fortunate it was that no member of our crew was a fussy eater. They were truly good sports, and accepted things as they came, lodging, food— even accidents! No one expected to find a Delmonico meal out in the wilds, miles from supplies. But any time we had the privilege of a home-cooked dinner (which occasionally we were invited to enjoy) we surely were *very* grateful and it was most welcome.

While we were still in the restaurant a series of heavy, sudden showers pelted down. The dark clay soil here could sop up huge quantities of water, gradually becoming a thick viscous mass, sticky as glue, and deep as your wheels could descend—at times, even deeper!

The men advised us to wait over in Rochelle; all hoped for clear weather on the morrow. Mr. Milks agreed to continue with us as far as Clinton, Iowa, across the Mississippi and to take "J.D." with him.

Somehow I had felt dog-tired today and was glad to quit early. Rising before daylight in Chicago for the Cobe Cup Races had set us back considerably in our quota of rest. Here was a chance to make up some of our sleep.

The brick hotel at Rochelle took care of us nicely and we started out refreshed for our entrance into what we regarded as the Real West. We felt the great Father of Waters was the logical division between the conservative, conventional East, with the busy hum of industries, and the wide-open spaces of the little-known West. In a matter of distance, we were still far from halfway, but there is a discernible difference in land and people once the Mississippi has been crossed.

Weather looked favorable as we went on through Dixon to Fulton, Illinois. A number of vehicles had gone over the road following the storm of the previous day, making a packed-down tread for our wheels. We were not often forced to pass an oncoming conveyance. When that did happen, we had to leave our smooth track, and slipped and slid, well-nigh powerless to direct our travel. The mud was so heavy that our skids could not reach a rapid rate of speed, but with flowing streams on either side of the highway, it would have been no trick at all to have landed the whole shebang in the ditch!

Eventually we saw ahead of us the superstructure of the bridge over the great river. Because of high waters caused by spring freshets and melting snows, the abutments began far back on shore and the bridge was of enormous length beyond the width of the river itself.[55] The floor of the bridge was of wood planking and just wide enough for passing. Altogether its width in proportion to its length looked pretty formidable, high above the wide water, and we were glad Mr. Milks' auto preceded us. It was rather scary to contemplate as we approached. What would we do if the engine failed in crossing?

Had our crew been a more loquacious one I'm sure the inside of the Maxwell just then would have sounded like the Tower of Babel for we were excited about this event in our journey. Instead, you could almost feel the tenseness of everyone. Silence reigned. It was a great emotional crisis. I had a pretty anxious time myself. But I kept reminding my subconscious mind that the bridge had been there for many springs and there was no reason why it should choose this particular time to collapse! The bridge obliged by reacting to such positive, trustful thinking, and we reached the other end of it in safety and with sincere relief. And thereby concluded a definite division of our Saga of Adventure.

Now, at last, we were *West*!

Crossing the Mississippi River from Fulton, Illinois, to Clinton, Iowa.

Notes

49. The Maxwell-Briscoe dealership was moved from 1407-09 S. Michigan Avenue to their new building at 1737 S. Michigan, sometime in 1909. The strip became known as "Motor Row." Several firms are at the latter location.
50. Alice probably would have driven to Geneva over Jackson, Washington, and Madison Roads, close to present Roosevelt Road, also Ill. 38. She had left the

route of the future Lincoln Highway in Valparaiso, but rejoined it in Geneva.

51. Al Hathaway, DDS, of Davenport, Iowa, owns the 10 millionth Model T Ford, which toured the country on the Lincoln Highway in 1924. When he commemorated the event in the same car sixty years later, he had many flats, caused mostly by pinched tubes due to improper remounting.

52. Despite a valiant effort by preservationists, DeKalb's historic post office was demolished in the 1990s, replaced by a Walgreens drug store.

53. Joseph F. Glidden's homestead, 921 W. Lincoln Way, is now a museum.

54. Alice probably stayed in Rochelle's Collier Inn, listed in the 1915 *Complete Official Road Guide of the Lincoln Highway*, with rates of $2 to $3 a night, with meals. It was located on the corner of Cherry Avenue and North Main Streets, a block or two east of the Lincoln Highway. The building was leveled in recent years, and the site is now a parking lot. The road through this part of Illinois was treacherous gumbo after a rain. Emily Post, on assignment for *Colliers* magazine, was delayed here by mud in 1915.

55. The east approach to the rickety old bridge was about a block north of "De Immigrant," the enormous Holland-built windmill erected in the 1990s to commemorate Fulton's Dutch heritage. The tough old bridge, built in 1891, was replaced in 1975.

6

The Mississippi River to Boone, Iowa

THE ROADS in Iowa were plainly a repetition of the kind we had in Western Illinois. We were doing quite well until we entered Mechanicsville. Then once more a sudden torrent descended upon us. We made quickly for the first shelter we could find. It proved to be the entrance to a livery stable, the door of which stood invitingly open.[56] As we drove inside, there were several buggies standing around, the horses still hitched to them. To say the animals were astonished to be joined by a horse-less carriage from which came the noise of a pulsating engine, is putting it mildly. There were a few hectic moments. We turned off the motor hurriedly and the stable gradually resumed its quieter mood. But the downpour went on and on, and we sat and waited for two full hours before we could stir out.

No need for anyone to tell us we could go no farther that day! We didn't even consider the question. Unwrapping our cases from the muddy covering and leaving the auto housed in the stable for the night, we made for the Page Hotel. It was a queer little place, but we were happy to take refuge in it. We ate supper in the City Restaurant with some country lads sitting at a couple of nearby tables. Over in one corner stood an ancient-vintage piano. The sight of four women gave the proprietor the inspiration and courage to ask one of us to play it. I could imagine what its tone would be; but I felt th urge to relieve the tension of the day's driving, so I casually tossed off a couple of light numbers. The lads gathered around and seemed to enjoy the "something different," and we went back to the hotel relaxed by the unexpected levity. It was to be expected that our youthful Hermine would enter into such a situation with fun, but it was always a pleasurable surprise to have my two conservative and almost haughtily reserved sisters-in-law react in similar fashion. But they took all things as they came and, in spite of the vexatious weather, they were beginning to get a certain thrill of adventure in our conquest of the Basin of Mud!

Naturally we had been disappointed in not reaching Cedar Rapids as we had planned for that day. After supper I attempted to telephone the Lattner Brothers who were agents for both the Maxwell and Ford autos, but the operator and I couldn't seem to get together. I don't know what the trouble was—maybe my Yankee language couldn't be understood in the Mid-West, but it was necessary for me to go over to the office and talk directly to the operator before we could arrive on common ground. When we got the connection to Cedar Rapids, Mr. Lattner offered to send a man over in the morning to show us the best way into town. D. A. Hiner was the one elected to do the job.

Before we could get away another thunderstorm added to the wretched condition of the gumbo roads.

"Does it always rain like this in Iowa?" I asked.

"Oh yes, at this time of the year. You got right smack into the rainy season," remarked a resident.

"Smack" was really the word for it. I'd heard of tropical rains that came down like that, but I was getting educated fast on the subject of rainfall within the United States. It took a certain amount of courage to set out each day knowing what *might* occur. If we had a little patience, the rain would quit finally and we would sally forth into the soppy highways.

It was my general policy to keep the gasoline tank at least half full. The 20-gallon reservoir was situated under the front seat cushion and there was no reading gauge for it. To check the contents it was necessary to empty the front compartment of personnel and cushion. Under both of these lay a wooden stick marked off in inches, which was plunged into the tank, revealing how many inches of fuel remained. The knowledge thus acquired was not necessarily dependably accurate but it was relatively so. In the hard driving and the downpours of the previous days this must have been neglected on my part. Just as we reached the top of a particularly long slippery hill, our motor choked, sputtered and ceased running. Much to my chagrin, we were out of gas! What a predicament! Was my face red?!

Poor Mr. Hiner walked back a mile and a half to the last farmhouse we had passed. He had noticed telephone wires leading in to the house. Thank goodness a few farmers had invested in that newest form of communication! He called Mr. Lattner, who saved the day—and us!—by bringing some gasoline.

In spite of these delays we reached Cedar Rapids in time for a wonderful luncheon at the Montrose Hotel—having covered but 25 miles.[57] We remained overnight in this town and enjoyed with our hosts the diversion of a sightseeing tour around the thriving metropolis.

We were thankful for this extra rest, for the following day was a terrible ordeal. Roads were horrible! The accumulated rains of the past several days had already soaked deep enough below the surface of the roads to render them bottomless. We plowed our way along, forced to keep the transmission in low gear most of the time. The water boiled, got low and needed replenishing before we could reach the next farm.[58]

What to do? We were not carrying extra water—it had been readily available before this. We began to wish we were on Noah's Ark with a real hull under us rather than this modern means of transportation intended only for dry land.

We could well understand the cry of the Ancient Mariner. "Water, water everywhere nor any drop to drink"—only we wanted ours in the radiator!

"There's plenty of water in the ditches beside us," said Maggie, "but how can we get it into the automobile? We have no pail."

True enough; but Nettie's ingenuity was equal to the occasion. "Can't we use the containers in our luggage?" She was referring to those handsome cutglass holders with sterling silver tops, for toothbrushes and other toilet articles—never designed to substitute for a common pail, either in size or ruggedness!

"Yes, I suppose we can," hesitatingly replied Maggie. "But they're awfully small."

"Well," Nettie went on, "it only means we take more trips to fill it up. Come on, let's get them out."

Can you picture those two sedate and dignified women in this performance? Without hesitation, they opened their treasured cases, removed the silver lids and contents of the beautiful cut-glass jars. Then, gathering up their ankle-length skirts, they stooped over to catch small amounts of water at a time and carried them repeatedly to the thirsty, yawning radiator! Back and forth, back and forth, they made countless trips before the height of the water was even visible as one peered into the opening. When at last they could see it, their efforts were spurred on. They never uttered a complaint about the job. They were contributing to the success of the journey in a very real way and were content. I don't know what we would have done without those little containers, not to mention the willing water-bearers who had the happy thought of putting them to use.

We were not blocking the road and no auto but ours was in sight. We had ample time to complete the operation. Of course, the water was not clean and clear, but it was water, and it was wet and cool. The engine was glad to have its new refreshment and purred at its former efficiency. But the heavy mud continued right with us and it wasn't long before we had the same problem to meet.

"Guess we'll have to put in more water. She's boiling again. Poor old motor," I said.

Out we piled and repeated "Operation Cut-Glass." This happened three times before we reached the next village where we could give the engine a few moments of well-earned rest and add to our supplies of water and oil. Then "on again, on again, rode the" four women!

A short distance beyond as we continued traveling at a slow pace, we approached a crossroads. At the far corner on the north side stood a large farm wagon driven by a lone woman in a sunbonnet. She had a beautiful team of well-fed horses; we stopped to pass the time of day with her.

Immediately she inquired: "Are you the women who are driving from New York to San Francisco?"

"Yes, we are," we answered as in one voice.

"I'm sure glad," she added. "I read about you in the paper and I've come six miles to see you and I've been waiting for a long time. Yes, I'm sure glad I saw you!"

We were very flattered by this encounter and told her how much we appreciated her telling us, waved goodbye, and started on. That little event gave us a special thrill. To think anyone would take that much trouble to see us go by! She must have possessed a lot of pioneer spirit herself!

How could *they make the Lincoln Highway out of that?*

We had gone but a few miles when a *real* detour now appeared before us. We were shunted completely off our road—(goodness knows what might have lain ahead!). First we traveled a mile north, then two or three miles west, before returning to our original route. The farmers on that particular piece of highway were evidently working out their poll tax by dumping "nice, new fill" to the depth of a foot. There was no way of avoiding it. It was exactly like driving through a deeply-plowed field of gumbo soil. The men still on the job stood aside to let us pass, their mouths literally agape with astonishment to see the auto pull through under its own power. As if that were not enough of a shock, their jaws dropped even lower when they realized we were all women!

We and the engine labored on. In negotiating those furrowed stretches it was fortunate that differentials were built nine or ten inches above ground level or we should have bogged down long since.

The "last straw" presented itself as we approached a small bridge over Weasel Creek. Ordinarily a tiny stream, it was now completely out of bounds, swollen by the repeated heavy storms.[59]

"Now what do we do?" asked Nettie.

"Well," I replied, "I can't tell how deep that water is and I don't intend to get stuck in the middle of it. I can wade in and see—provided I can stand up in the slippery mess."

Maggie suggested cautiously, "Maybe we better pull off to the side and stay here until it subsides."

It wasn't raining now so we thought there was little chance of the water rising higher than it already was. The road was narrow but at the left there was an area wide enough for the auto to stand without obstructing the passage of another vehicle—if any! We drew out of the traveled rut and prepared to remain overnight.

Donning my boots, I removed my suit skirt. The girls watched curiously while I yanked up my slip and pulled it forward between my legs as an Arab brings his long garment from back to front to form bloomers. It wasn't beautiful but it was a way to explore the situation without getting wet all over—so long as I could stay upright. Grabbing my umbrella to help in maintaining my equilibrium in the muck, I stepped gingerly into the edge of the creek. It was an acrobatic feat just to remain standing. I didn't wade in very far, just far enough to make certain we couldn't go on at the present.

"Let's make a little supper and see how things are later," said I. The hamper with its limited supplies was now pressed into service. We were in need of bread and water and Hermine offered to walk back to the nearest farm to see if we could purchase them. They cost the large sum of twenty-five cents—plus a hasty retreat from a large litter of scuttling black pigs!

As we ate our impromptu snack on the only patch of long grass big enough to hold our "tea party," Hermine, somewhat in the manner of Pollyanna remarked: "This isn't too bad."

No, it wasn't, considering the circumstances. And it wasn't very good, either. But give Hermine "E" for effort—she was trying to help us keep up

61

our morale!

It takes a situation like this to make one appreciative of simple fare. We were all properly thankful and grateful, I'm sure.

Dusk came on. The water still showed no sign of receding. So we gathered up our paraphernalia, mumbling that we guessed we'd have to sleep right here, and dolefully climbed back into our seats.

The girls had voted to change places in the automobile as we drove along from day to day—all but the driver, of course. I was just stuck in one spot for the duration. It so happened that that day Hermine was in front with me and the sisters in back. The top was raised and the curtains attached; also the piece which acted as a windshield was down in front. The only relief from a sitting position for the driver was putting both booted feet up on the dashboard. With head leaning back against the upright rib of the top—and boy, was it hard!—I spent the hours of darkness. Hermine was welcome to the rib on the opposite side!

And I slept with my feet on the dash and the steering wheel poking me in the abdomen, until barking hounds awakened us.

Remember the pillows someone inquired about when we were leaving New York? This is the one place where we could have used a quartette of them. But where would we have kept them all the rest of the time?

It wasn't going to be easy to sleep all night with a steering wheel poking into my abdomen with no chance to change position! But the exhaustion caused by driving for hours through that heavy mud, hanging on to a wheel stubbornly resisting me all the while (no power-steering then) proved to be a blessing in disguise, for I believe I slept for several hours.

Suddenly we were all awakened by the piercing noise of barking dogs. There had been no passing of man or beast—or auto—since we settled down for the night. Now we were all on the alert instantly. What was going on? It came nearer and nearer, until in the half-light of pre-dawn we could barely discern four baying hounds splashing through the watery mud beside us. What were they after? Would it attempt to seek refuge with us or—let's hope—keep right on going? Well, they never slowed down by foot or voice and passed by us on a dead run. I hope the poor prey made good his escape. They afforded us both excitement and amusement, in spite of lessening our time for sleep.

As morning dawned about four, we noticed a decided abatement of the water and could distinguish continuous road ahead, furrowed as it still was with countless rivulets.

With our little Sterno outfit we soon prepared a very simple breakfast and started on our way.[60] The road was awful, of course, but we did pull through it and were glad to be in motion once more. Before eight, we arrived in Belle Plaine where we supplemented our scanty meal with a *real* breakfast at Herring Cottage.[61] My! *that* was good! When the family learned we had spent the night beside Weasel Creek—if not quite *in* it—the man sympathetically proffered a bag of delicious cherries—"to keep the wolf from the door!"

All of the moisture of the past few days had taken its toll on the ignition system; before long there was a skip in the motor. In a four-cylinder engine there's not much doubt about such a fact! Climbing down, I discovered the offending spark plug by the simple trick of holding a hammer head against each one and shorting it against the water jacket of the cylinders. Plugs were manufactured then so they could be taken apart, cleaned with fine sandpaper or emery cloth and reassembled, which I did on the spot. It was a dirty job but didn't involve too much time. The girls were interested in watching the process, so the time passed rapidly and we were soon on our way again. I could only wipe off the grime with a rag—no chance for a real clean-up until later. What would I not have given for the facilities of a modern filling station after such a business!

From here our route lay through the Tama Indian Reservation to Marshalltown, where we took time for lunch. None of us had ever seen so many Indians before and we were thrilled by the new experience.[62]

With the cessation of the rain and the partial drying of the roads, Iowa was looking up a bit in our estimation as we neared Boone, a little more than halfway across the state. Maybe our ardent wishes for the rain to stop had actually come to fruition, at least until we could get beyond the Missouri River.

Whoops! I spoke too soon! Another torrent of rain. We put into the Northwestern Hotel on a run, glad to escape the worst of the storm.[63]

Boone is forever emblazoned on our minds as the scene of The Great Temptation!

The lobby of the hotel alongside the railroad tracks was filled with guests and local residents, mostly men, curious and interested in our trip. And advice was flowing freely.

"If I were you women," came a gratuitous expression of opinion, "I'd put that Maxwell on a flat car and ship it down to Omaha. This isn't going to get any better until you're over the Missouri River about a hundred miles."

"Sure would," a bystander agreed.

"Yes, sirree," added another.

"That's right," was heard all around. The vote seemed to be unanimous.

For a weak moment I was tempted by indecision. We surely were fed up with Iowa mud and the rain. Am I foolish to go on? Am I just being stubborn? Should I heed this well-meant "Voice of Experience" warning?

No! "Get thee behind me, Satan." I'll drive every inch of the way if it kills me! To me it would have been "cheating" of a sort to use railroad transportation for part of the journey across the continent. The girls concurred in my viewpoint.

"It's up to you. You're the captain. We'll stick with you," said Nettie, and the others affirmed her expression. I was pleased that they felt confidence in my conclusion.

We did wish that the weather would give us a break, however, and for a few days *stop raining!!*

Notes

56. Alice would have crossed the C&NW tracks carefully on the graded dirt road. The Page Hotel, at 219 First St., was passed to get the livery stable, 211 First Street, remodeled a long time ago into Bubba's, a saloon today. The hotel was three doors east of there. It was remodeled into the Page Apartments about 1959. The travelers would have walked to the City Restaurant at 215 First Street from the hotel. That building is now a chiropractor's office.

57. The Montrose Hotel was razed about 1990. It stood on the corner of 3rd Avenue and 3rd Street SE, one to two blocks north of the Lincoln Highway. One of the better hotels in 1909, the rates were $1.50 up. The Lincoln came through downtown Cedar Rapids on First Avenue until the late teens, when it was moved over to Second Avenue.

58. Alice has been driving the muddiest stretches of the road that would become the Lincoln Highway—coast to coast.

59. Weasel Creek flows beneath a small bridge on present US 30. It is 1.5 miles west of Youngville, where Highway 218 leaves US 30 to head north.

60. Sterno®, a portable cooking fuel, was introduced about 1900 and still is used to warm buffet serving trays and chafing dishes.

61. Herring Cottage is now Herring Apartments, still standing on the north side of the Lincoln Highway, Thirteenth and Eighth Avenue, in the center of Belle Plaine.

62. Tama is still home to the tribe, now known as Musquakie.

63. Boone's Northwestern Hotel was located in the old Chicago and Northwestern Railroad depot, at Ninth and Keeler Streets. This is one block west of Story Avenue and a block north. The depot was razed in 1969.

7

Boone to Vail, Iowa

THERE WERE approximately 150 miles between Boone, Iowa, and Omaha, Nebraska, across from Council Bluffs on the Missouri River.

We were aware that the western part of Iowa became somewhat more hilly, which meant we would probably have more dry road; but we had also been warned of several pretty bad stretches and a very steep hill just beyond the town of Jefferson. This was known as Danger Hill, and autos using it were often obliged to turn around and climb it in reverse gear. That was a nice prospect for the day's drive![64]

We supplemented what information we already had by questioning reliable residents of the local scene at Boone, who were well acquainted with the route to Omaha. They thought we were too heavily loaded with our four passengers and extra equipment and luggage to attempt the trip to Omaha under these flood conditions. If we would not consider shipping the automobile by rail, they strongly advised us to lighten it as much as possible.

The four of us talked the matter over in conference with "J.D."

"What do you think?" I inquired of the others.

"I guess you *must* lighten the Maxwell, if there's any way to do it," said "J.D."

"Well," said Nettie, "since you intend going by way of Omaha, the three of us could go there by train, and "J.D." could remain behind and ride with you. If there's any kind of emergency he would be able to give you more valuable help than any of us could."

"But that wouldn't decrease the weight by much more than a hundred pounds, since "J.D." must weigh almost as much as you and Maggie together," I remarked, laughing.

"How about me?" put in Hermine. She was the tallest of the three and of rather robust build. "My weight counts for a good bit."

"That's right," said I. "And now I think of it, there are those two spare springs, bolted to the running board, we haven't had to use yet. They surely weigh a lot. Maybe we could ship those to Omaha by rail."

"You don't think that's foolish?" asked Maggie, a trifle nervously.

"Well, I can't think of anything that would relieve the weight more, and I guess we just better take the chance. We almost *have* to," I added, in desperation.

"And the three suitcases will help a *little* more, too," said Maggie as an afterthought.

I realized not taking the springs was quite a gamble. With all this water running down the valley toward the big city, there could be some bad washouts and deep chuck holes, any one of which might well snap a spring leaf. Then I comforted myself with the idea that perhaps it wouldn't be so likely to occur with the lighter burden. We just *had* to risk it!

"I hate to have you girls sacrifice part of the ride to do that," I ventured after mulling it over. Maybe I was feeling a little sorry for myself to be separated from my feminine pals.

"You're the one who's making the sacrifice this time, I'd say," answered Maggie.

"No, I don't feel that way at all. It's part of my job," I replied.

"We understand how *you* feel," said Nettie, "but the main thing is to get the Maxwell through, and anything *we* can do to achieve that is little enough. Besides, you'll probably make it in a day or two and then we'll get aboard and go on from there."

They all seemed determined to handle it that way; so in the morning we shipped the springs and put the girls on the train before "J.D." and I started off in the same direction by road. We would reach there as soon as possible and we put out with high hopes for good fortune. However, all this shifting of plans had consumed time and it was one o'clock before we left Boone.

A bad piece of road east of Jefferson got us stuck in one awful hole from which we were towed by Charles Clark of Beaver. It was four in the afternoon when we arrived at Jefferson. There had been no opportunity for dinner and the Adrians and Haags were expecting us. Mr. Haag was really the banker in Jefferson but, with his friend Mr. Adrian, he had taken on the Maxwell agency as a sideline. The two couples and the Haags' little daughter Pauline were more than hospitable to us and insisted on preparing dinner in their lovely home at four-thirty. This wonderful kindness brought us nostalgic sentiments as we dined once more in a private home with such friendly people.

Mr. Haag was deeply interested in the Good Roads Movement and worked hard to secure backing for the project. Goodness knows! The state of Iowa needed all the assistance of consecrated men it could muster. This was the route which later became the Lincoln Highway—I almost feel as if I were the "Mother" of it! And, believe me, the labor pangs prior to its birth were terrific! It is still a lusty and worthy offspring—even if its name is now obscured and desecrated by its unromantic designation as Route 30!

Leaving Jefferson, we soon encountered Danger Hill.[65] This is a climb dreaded by all, since there is a ninety degree turn at the bottom, preventing any advantage which might be gained by making a run for it. After we made the turn and started up the muddy grade we saw ahead of us, possibly two-thirds of the way up, another automobile. The driver was having a difficult time of it as he tried again and again to go forward. Finally his motor coughed, spit, and stopped. The man and woman got out and looked about them. She mounted the bank beside the road and he got out a shovel and tried to rid the wheels of some of the accumulated mud. Then he resumed his seat, started the engine and tried again. It chugged and chugged, slipped about a bit, and stalled. Again he tried, but could get no traction.

I had waited below to give him a chance to get out of the way. It was now apparent that he would remain there for some time unless he received outside help. Fortunately his brakes held and he did not slide down from his original position—I had been watching anxiously for that.

There was no one in sight but us. I suggested to "J.D." that we offer to tow him. "J.D." agreed and called out to the driver: "We have a rope. Do you want us to pull you up?"

"Oh, would you?" he asked eagerly.

"We'll try," I replied. "Fasten the rope to the front of your Mitchell and I'll try to come by you and get into position so you can tie to the Maxwell," I said.

The woman hopefully watched from the bank as they carried out my instructions. I started up the motor, let in the clutch slowly and the auto responded as I gently and carefully squeezed by the other vehicle.

Then, as they tied to the Maxwell, I continued, "Start *your* motor, too, and put it in low gear. That will relieve my engine of your dead weight. I'll signal you when I'm starting ahead." I was very willing to tow his Mitchell but I didn't want the extra strain of a dead weight besides.

It was slippery going, all right, but the chains kept us on the road. Going by him wasn't as fearsome as backing down into position to tie on. If the Maxwell began sliding, it might crash into his radiator. Our engine had wonderful compression and by allowing it to drift back *very* slowly, we made a "perfect landing." Once tied together and the slack in the line taken up, I signalled him for the start upgrade. As the clutch engaged I felt the heavy pull on the motor and fed it extra gas to compensate for the additional load. This is a delicate operation which necessitates balancing exactly the amount of gas fed to the motor with the burden put upon it.

The two vehicles moved ahead as one—slowly but surely up the remainder of Danger Hill. After we had passed the crest, there were exchanges of thanks and farewells and we proceeded toward Carroll, proud to think the sturdy Maxwell had not only made the grade itself but had rescued the other travelers besides.

The road from here to Vail had one section composed of a veritable sea of chuck holes of varying sizes, most of them so filled with water that it was difficult to determine their depths. This experience with mud holes was fast becoming a specialized education. Eventually we learned to estimate the depths of them fairly accurately by the comparative slopes of the edges of the puddles.

All of a sudden I heard "J.D." say, "Gosh all hemlock, isn't that something." Ahead lay a particularly evil-looking stretch.

"It certainly is!" was my reply, "but there's no way of ducking it. I'll try to ride the ridges as much as I can. Here goes! Hang on!"

One deep and muddy chuck hole wrecks our progress.

We crawled along, picking our path cautiously. Sometimes the ridge was flat and broad enough to make a fair footing between the bowls of muddy water. Would it continue?

It was impossible to avoid all the holes with all four wheels.

The Maxwell careened back and forth, diving in one direction, then another. If we could conquer this section without snapping a spring first we might make it. I began to doubt whether this was the right day to have shipped those springs after all! Well, we did our best when we made our decision. "Angels could do no more!" Speaking of angels, I wouldn't be surprised if a little silent prayer went up for help in this crisis.

Dodge a hole! Catch a breath! Now another! and another! So far so good.

O-O-ooo that ridge looks a trifle narrow. Can we make it? We are almost past it when

Plop! the rear end starts slipping to the right and into the hole we plunge! It's a deep one, too! We're hung up on the differential housing and the suspended wheel churns up the water like a paddle wheel, only helplessly!

"J.D." and I looked at each other forlornly. What to do now? No one around! But our guardian angels were right behind us with their hovering assistance, thank heaven. That hole was most strategically located. Right beside the road was a pile of sturdy fence rails! What a godsend for us!

While I considered the best method of working out our difficulty, "J.D." said, "Do you suppose if I pried with one of those fence rails under that rear tire, it would give you enough traction to pull out?"

There wasn't a thing to do but try. He stood a good chance of a sudden and thorough bath of gumbo mud. But he was a game, self-effacing assistant.

I wondered if he had noticed the front wheel was also in a hole. So I said "I believe if we jack up the front wheel to remove the resistance of forcing it out of the hole first, the rail against the rear tire *would* do it."

It seemed quite impossible to find a flat and dry enough spot to set the jack base so it would hold under the axle when raised. Ah yes, the shovel! Laying the metal part down, it made a good foundation on which to operate the jack, and we raised the front end of the suffering Maxwell until it was in a regular contortion!

We also tried attaching the rope to the front axle and yanking the front end over so it would fall off the jack clear of the hole. That did help in that spot, but to get out entirely we would have to have traction at the rear wheels or a pair of percherons! Perhaps if the force were applied in the correct place, we could do the trick with *one* percheron (namely, "J.D.") and the sturdy fence rail! Picking up one from the pile and placing it under the tire, "J.D." and all the avoirdupois he possessed pushed hard, as I let in the clutch to add the Maxwell's bit. I was glad at that moment for every pound of weight our "courier" had and for all thirty "horses" in the Maxwell!

Covering faithful "J.D." with glory as well as with mud, the Maxwell fairly leapt with joy as she lifted herself once more onto terra firma—not too "firma" to be sure.

At the rate we were proceeding we wouldn't make Omaha very fast.

When we entered the tiny settlement of Vail, the lower street was a shambles. Two days before it had been hit by a terrific flood, leaving the board sidewalks so buckled they could scarcely be used. Water a foot deep still stood in some of the stores and shops. It was a pathetic sight!

Most of the water, to be sure, had run down the valley toward Council Bluffs and the residents in Vail doubted if we could get through beyond Denison. They seemed pretty positive about it. This broke up our original plan completely. We needed to hold a conference—and we were also anxious to get mail at Omaha—so we decided to take the train and join the girls at the Hotel Rome.

While we waited for train time, we entertained ourselves watching the telegraph operator. We grew hungry at last but there was no restaurant in town.

"Come on," said "J.D.", "let's see what we can find in the little grocery store."

The owner proved to be sympathetic and ingenious. Soon we were seated on a couple of wooden crates, with a large piece of wrapping paper on a third box for a table and cloth. We had crackers and cheese and sardines, using toothpicks for forks. We were fed; we had fun as well—and we boarded the train for the ride to the big city.

The girls were delighted to see us, but totally unprepared for the news of our present situation. They had been expecting us— but, *in* the Maxwell!

It happened that Mr. W. S. Hathaway, District Manager of the Maxwell-Briscoe Company at Kansas City, and Mr. Rooklidge of the same city, were in Omaha. This was most fortunate for us as the Omaha agent turned out to be most discourteous and disagreeable and would not give us any help. This was the only occurrence of the kind we encountered on the entire journey. Perhaps the District Manager knew of his methods and was on hand to look out for us.

Conferring with these two gentlemen, it was deemed best to give up the whole idea of driving through Omaha and instead to take the automobile from Vail to Denison, thence northwestward to Sioux City, which stood on higher ground. There we would cross the Missouri River into Nebraska and work gradually back to our original route at Columbus. Since we should be able to go from Vail to Sioux City in a day, with any luck, the girls preferred to go by rail to the latter city and join us there. Before our departure, Mr. Hathaway had gotten Mr. Groves, the agent at Sioux City, to promise to send his excellent man, Eugene Gnehm, to show us the way.

With this fine assistance in view, "J.D." and I boarded the train and returned to Vail and the awaiting Maxwell.

Notes

64. Those early automobiles had no fuel pumps, and the gasoline was fed to the carburetor by gravity. However, backing up steep hills also gave the advantage of reverse gear transmission bands, which always had less wear than the forward bands.

65. Danger Hill was just west of the Raccoon River bridge. The hill is much tamer today, but the left turn at the bottom is still there.

8

Vail to Cheyenne, Wyoming

WITH THE arrival of Eugene Gnehm from Sioux City, the three of us started back to his home town. Everything seemed to be working in fine shape. We had gone but three miles when there was a sudden loss of power as we began to mount a slight grade. The left side of the auto settled into a slant position—and the wheel quietly rolled off into the long grass. Me, oh my! The rear axle had broken! And finding the missing wheel would be like playing "Button, button, who's got the button?" Now we were stuck for some time.[66]

Gene telephoned to Mr. Groves who said he would ship an axle, which should arrive on the 7:15 a.m. train.

Not wishing to leave the auto unattended on the road, and unable to move it off to the side, I spent the entire day under an improvised tent made by arranging my duster over some roadside bushes. I occupied myself writing up my diary and expense accounts. The summer sun was *hot*—the kind that makes the Iowa corn grow eight or nine feet high when assisted by that rainy season we have mentioned.

Mr. Boylan frorn Denison employed a man to sleep in the car for the night as a watchman, and brought us to Denison where there was a hotel.[67] Back out to the Maxwell at seven in the morning via Mr. McCulloch's team, I went to await the coming of the axle, only to learn it had been lost by an inexperienced express agent and couldn't possibly get there before evening or the following morning; so back to town I went. Later Gene sent word that it was ready. To make up for this extra delay, we rose at 5 a.m. and, with a cruller and coffee inside, went back to the Maxwell for a fresh start. We supplemented our insufficient breakfast in Denison with reinforcement against further possible emergencies ahead—we were learning to be very cautious about what might lie ahead—and were on the road once more at eight.

All was not smooth sailing, however. Twice we had to be towed out of holes. A good bit of the road surface here was dry enough so chains were not necessary all the time; but every once in a while we would strike a real big mud puddle in a hollow, where the water was unable to run off. And there we would stick. Gene attempted to walk through one of the puddles, slipped and fell, and had an involuntary mud bath. He had been unable to use my boots. Wrong size!

The little Sioux River had broken its bounds and a rut pulled our front wheels into the water before we realized what was happening. The Maxwell was viciously slanted off to the left, with a chance it might tip over. On the front seat between "J.D." and me lay my handbag.—But not for long!

As we lurched toward the overflowing water, off the seat with accelerated speed went the purse! Quick as a flash, "J.D." made a grab for it but failed to connect. Fortunately the bag floated and without a word or hesitation his foot shot out in its direction. He cleverly worked his foot into the strap as he braced himself between the dash and the back of the seat. He landed the bag without casualty for the purse had not been in contact with the water long enough to wet the contents, thank goodness! Travelers' cheques do not work well when damp.

Running in a generally northwesterly direction, we crossed several streams rushing to join the Missouri River with their overburdened waters. We made fair time through Mapleton and Smithland, toward our reunion with the girls. It was going to feel mighty good to have our party intact once more. I think they were as joyful to see us as we were to return to them.

The date of our reaching Sioux City was Friday, July second, and we hoped to arrive at Columbus by the fifth. The Fourth fell on Sunday that year. It would be a special celebration for us to be back on our route again.

The H. B. Groves and the George Jamessons were our fine hosts at the Country Club where we spent a delightful evening. I'm afraid we did most of the talking as they wanted to hear about our trip so far.

We didn't need to use strong language about their roads and their rainy season. The natives had the same idea! We could say with sincerity we thought Iowa a beautiful, prosperous, rolling state—the prettiest we had seen since Pennsylvania—in spite of the multiplicity of misfortunes we had had in it. The people were so eager for us to like their state, to which they had great loyalty. And we really did like it; but—oh, those terrible roads!!

Eons ago this entire section between the Mississippi and Missouri Rivers had been submerged. The residents often referred to it as "river bottoms." This seemed a good term except that, in places, it was hard to believe it had any bottom. It does grow wonderful farm crops but—unpaved—it was never recommended for motoring. We were convinced by this time that we would have no fine sailing until we had passed the Missouri by nearly 100 miles. So our anxiety to attain that goal was exceedingly keen.

Spending the night in Mr. Groves' garage, the Maxwell once more was cleansed of a load of gumbo and made ready for the Nebraska journey. The mud had eaten considerable paint from the wheels, which was not noticeable until the gumbo was removed. When we finished each day's drive, it looked as if we had two tires, one within the other on each wheel, one of rubber, the other of gray mud, to match.

The girls took this opportunity to repair the ravages of the first three weeks with personal washing, shampooing, etc., before they felt comfortable to depart. In spite of our ardent desire to continue, we forfeited one more day for this purpose. I purchased a new duster in the metropolis. Mine had surely seen better days, from its trials and tribulations of the road.

On the morrow we were ready to go. Just as we were setting out for the garage, it began to *pour* in good old Iowa fashion. Inside of an hour so much rain had fallen it was inadvisable to think of going that day. More "kicking of heels" and "just settin'." Disgusted, we made our way back to the West Hotel and waited and waited, mostly in discouraged idleness.[68] We were glad we had received mail from home in Omaha; we had to read and re-read it for solace. It would have been wonderful if transcontinental telephoning could have brought us the voices of our loved ones at home, at that particular spot in the journey. We had many nostalgic moments but had to keep on going, so we pocketed our feelings and read the letters once more.

"J.D." left for Columbus next morning by train to await our coming.

The following morning showed no improvement in the weather and by this time I was champing at the bit to be on our way. I displayed my irritation at the inertia of the situation by remarking, "Well, I don't think things are going to get any better while we remain here. I'm for going on tomorrow."

One of the residents had sought to dissuade us from leaving the city by saying, "Up the street is the toll bridge to the Nebraska side of the river. If you will just take a nickel and go across that bridge and look at the piece of road on the other side, I think you'll change your mind about starting."[69]

Now almost at my wit's end with frustration and impatience due to the repeated downpours and our difficult experiences, I replied:

"I don't mind spending the nickel, but I just don't think we will have any good luck until we get out of Iowa. I hate to say that, but it *has* been pretty bad. I don't want to *see* that stretch of road. If there is anyone who will pilot us through it, I'm for going on." The girls were in accord.

At this point Mr. Groves offered to have Eugene Gnehm precede the Maxwell through that terrible part. Gene was an excellent mechanic, I knew, and I believed he would do a fine job getting us past this awful spot. We decided to trust his guidance.

The Fourth and its celebration on Monday had already fled into the past when we set out the next afternoon at three. Gene and Mr. Jamesson pulled out in the lead and we crossed the bridge. That was easy. Immediately beyond lay this terrific piece of roadway. It wasn't much worse-looking than the one where "J.D." was obliged to use the fence rail to extricate us—but the girls hadn't seen *that* one, since they were not with us when we negotiated it. Both autos could only crawl along in low gear, picking their way very gingerly. *We* had the advantage of seeing where *not* to go by the motion of the vehicle ahead—and we knew enough to remain behind them. Suddenly Gene's auto came to a dead stop and he turned off his motor. What had happened? He was done for. Something in his differential had broken and he was unable to move. Only horses could get him out of this predicament. We waited while they procured a team which towed him back to the garage. They advised our employing the same method to avoid a similar disaster, so we stayed right there until the horses and driver returned. They towed us the remaining distance through this frightful section, then went on to Jackson under our own power.

Though we had covered but 13 miles, all this delay had consumed a great deal of time and it was seven in the evening when we turned into the little village. We found a little "peanut" of a hotel where all four of us had to sleep in one room.[70] We had to perch on stools at the tiny restaurant counter; but we were so grateful to find a place to eat and sleep that we were not critical—but highly amused. In spite of the simplicity of our accommodations, we spent a delightful evening with the Kearney family and Dr. Leahy. When we returned to the hotel, we discovered there were no street lights and it was far from easy to find our way. Stumbling through the darkness, we giggled and giggled as we made our way back. Oh, for a flashlight at that point! The Maxwell was occupying primitive lodgings also—again in a livery stable.

When our road turned toward the south some miles after Jackson we saw we would not be going *westward* from the Missouri River very fast. But there were some hills and a few dry spots, so our expectancy grew with each mile. Mr. Kearney and Dr. Leahy had accompanied us as far as Vista—just a house and a grain elevator—and put us on the road to Allen.[71] We had some trouble with the water circulation in the radiator and had to stop repeatedly to add to its supply; even so, we reached Allen for lunch. Here we were directed to an apartment over a cigar store for a place to eat.

We spent a large part of this day in second gear, but were inspired by the fact that our mileage edged up a lot—from 13 to 36 miles. It took 12 hours to do it, too; but we arrived at Wisner for the night.[72] This drive which we hoped to run off in one day, from Sioux City to Columbus, was taking us a good deal more. What would "J.D." think of our failure to arrive?

We were "ripe" for any form of encouragement. The water supply was remedied somewhat by the gift of a jug—and I do mean a jug—probably the kind that had been used for corn whiskey, from its appearance. In this the donor placed an adequate cork, with these words: "Now," with a twinkle in his eye at the thought, "you have a Nebraska jug with an Iowa cork. That ought to bring you good luck!"

We were grateful for the jug; but I wondered if we were not a trifle tongue-in-cheek as to the cork. It would be a long time before we would look upon *any* article from Iowa as a token of good luck, I suspected. Thirteen days had been consumed getting across its 360 miles of gumbo from east to west!

But so far, Nebraska's reputation wasn't too good, either. We were towed out of two holes in the distance of a mile. The farmer's son caught one of their horses in pasture and pulled us out—for a fee—then walked on to the next hole, repeated his towing but *doubled* his fee! It was well for us there were no more puddles in that vicinity if he figured on working with such mathematics.

The day had been a cloudy one and the road was a poor thoroughfare in a sparsely populated section. Six miles of it had been worked on and it was heavy with loose soil. When we came to a long slippery hill we were lucky to receive an invitation from two well-diggers with a sturdy team and wagon to "tote" the girls up the grade. The Maxwell, thus relieved of several hundred pounds, made it easily. At the top I took back my cargo of amused passengers.

A couple of friendly well-diggers lighten our load in more ways than one.

"Surely we will reach Columbus tomorrow," we sighed each night. We could see a tiny bit of improvement each day in the condition of the roads, though occasional stretches brought new despair to our hearts. After the first 12 miles of heavy and rough roadway, I found that the screws in the magneto plate had loosened and one had fallen out and could not be found. It was a mean spot to reach, but I tightened the others as well as I could and they held. Then the spring on the foot brake pedal, under the floor, broke and I was obliged to get under the auto and fix it with a piece of wire. After that, we went along fairly well. It had gotten on to two o'clock and we had had no lunch. As we passed a farmhouse, Hermine said, "Do you think we might be able to get some bread and drinking water from that house and fix something to eat?" I had been struggling with these other difficulties and had completely forgotten about food. There had been no chance to stop at any kind of restaurant, for we had passed through no towns. As soon as I realized the situation, I drew up at the grassy roadside. With some fruit we were carrying, we had an adequate enough meal. As we sat there consuming it, the rural mail-carrier came by and stopped to chat. He noticed the New Jersey license and said "Have you four ladies driven all the way from New Jersey?" He was even more surprised when he learned we were going to the Pacific Coast. He thought he would rather have his 29 miles of Nebraska dirt roads on a mail route than to have to do what we had set out to accomplish. It was hard to tell where the advantage lay! Twenty-nine miles of these roads all year round would really be something!

We had to admit the "highway" *was* actually improving, however, as we went farther away from the Missouri River. At Howells, we were advised to take the route to Leigh and come directly into Columbus from the north, rather than go into the old road at Fremont and thence westward.[73] This was both because of a better road and the presence of a good Maxwell agent, Mr. Hoesley, in that town. Those two items of news were welcome! The hotel wasn't much, but it *was* clean.[74]

The four of us were talking together in one front room just after we reached our second floor accommodations. At the front side there was a door looking out upon a tiny balcony. As I stepped to the doorway to look out, there was so little protection that I felt as if I might be propelled to the ground again. Down below, at the side of the entrance to the building, stood a row of stiff-legged chairs. Two of these, tipped back against the front of the hotel, held men in shirt sleeves and suspenders, who well might have been plowing a field some time earlier. One said to the other, "Say, did yer see them four women who came in a while ago? Drove an auto*mo*bile all the way from New York and they're aimin' to git ter California! Come on in the dinin' room and see if they're there."

I hated to eavesdrop but this was too good to miss. So I kept on listening.

"I've seen 'em," was the blasé reply. And that was that! In the little village of Leigh our stock was not very high. I suspect his interest in horseless carriages had not yet been aroused—and he certainly wasn't putting himself out for women!

But he couldn't knock pride out from under us with that retort. We had triumphed by piling up the staggering total of 51 miles. Hurrah for the champion Maxwell and the gradually-improving roads!

Turning south at the Creston Cemetery we came directly into Columbus and back on our route as originally scheduled. Here we found "J.D.," so happy to see us once more—this time only a couple of days late.[75]

After lunch we wanted to press on to Grand Island to make up some of the lost time. Nettie was not feeling too well and preferred to take the train and meet us there. Now that we had come this far into Nebraska, the roads had a very noticeable gravelly content, allowing us to run along more smoothly and make much better speed. The second and low gears had taken over for so long a time that we almost forgot the Maxwell had a third or high gear. After its lengthy rest, it was full of energy.

Nettie waved to us from the train as it pulled away. We set out to catch her after our own fashion. It was only a matter of 65 miles, and what is that if roads are getting better!

Within ten miles of Grand Island we were overtaken by a fierce rain-and-hail storm. Black, black clouds brought with them a tremendous wind and we were loath to continue. At the north side of the road stood a farmhouse, and we pulled in and brought the auto to a stop on the lee side of the good-looking house. The family came out to invite us in while the storm continued. When we entered and began to talk, we discovered they were a family of Danes who could speak no English. We couldn't understand each other, but I'm sure we imparted to them our gratitude for their hospitality. The storm passed without too much delay and we joined Nettie at six-fifteen—

81

The Geiger family were mighty kind to us at Grand Island, Nebraska.

our mileage boosted to 92! Without any mishaps, every day in every way we were getting a little bit better.

Nettie had improved enough to ride on with us in the morning. Four miles from Grand Island the first mishap came along. The right half of the rear axle broke!

There's nothing like a broken axle to put one completely out of business for the time being. It occurred right by the farm of Mr. Geiger. They were all sympathetically hospitable to us and Mr. Geiger conveyed us all back to town in his lumber wagon behind a handsome team of black horses. "J.D." had not yet left Grand Island, so he phoned to the Fernald Auto Company, state representatives in Denver, Colorado, for a mechanic and a new axle. H. H. Miller came out by train with the axle and the two of us went back to the scene and installed it in the auto, finishing the job at 9 p.m. He thought the magneto needed some attention, so instead of going on the following morning, we spent considerable time cleaning and overhauling it.

This was to be quite a stretch to Cheyenne, climbing into the foothills leading us to the Great Divide. When we were talking it over, Nettie said, "Why don't I go on by train to Cheyenne with "J.D." and let Mr. Miller take my place in the Maxwell? That's a particularly open piece of country, especially beyond North Platte. He has to go back in that direction to return to Denver, so it won't be much out of his way."

Mr. Miller was an excellent mechanic and was used to working on Maxwells, so it seemed a good idea. We decided to try it. After all the cleaning we had done on the automobile, we left Grand Island at four that afternoon, hoping to make Lexington for the night stop. West of Kearney, when we were about two miles beyond Elm Creek Station, we lodged in a slimy mud hole from which we could not escape without assistance. The main part of the road had been so good that we were not wearing tire chains. We remembered we had passed some shacks occupied by men grading the railroad. Walking back, we secured the services of a man and his horse to tow us out—while the four or five families living there watched the operation from the sidelines.

We didn't reach Lexington, but got as far as Overton, where the family of the agent, W. H. Hill, took us all into their home for the night with warm and genial hospitality. In the morning, their son, Clare, and his mother escorted us to Lexington, about 12 miles farther on.

Since returning to our original route at Columbus we had remained on the north side of the Platte River. This stream has its source in eastern Wyoming, flows across the entire state of Nebraska and joins the Missouri River below Omaha.[76] As we entered the town of North Platte, we crossed the river on a long wooden bridge, on the sides of which we could read the name of the store where we might purchase good "men's suits" in town! Just what four women wanted![77] Our way kept on westerly toward the Rockies and the capital of Wyoming. This was the old Overland Stage route of years ago and we could not help thinking how much slower was their travel than ours.

Our Maxwell had been so shaken up with its strenuous journey that numerous bolts had loosened and some minor troubles developed. We adjusted a few important ones and kept on climbing the lower foothills toward

Our hospitable Hill family at Overton, Nebraska.

the glorious mountains of the Rocky range. We were progressing well enough; the grades were not too great as yet, though some were rather heavy with sand—not too unlike the Montauk Point dunes! It looked as if we would reach Chappell, anyway. Entering Ogallala, we saw a group of men and horses. Some of the men were in uniform, of a sort. Advancing before us, one of the men held up his hand, signalling us to stop. It looked too formidable a crowd to be a hold-up, though the idea crossed my mind at first. No matter—it meant *stop*! So—we stopped!

"What's the matter? What's going on?" I inquired of the man who appeared to be in charge.

He paid no attention to my question, but started on some of his own.

"Where yer comin' from?" he asked, a trifle gruffly, I thought.

"From New York," I replied. I believe he expected the name of a

84

Bridge over the Platte River at North Platte, Nebraska.

town nearer by.

"We're on our way to San Francisco," I added. This certainly must have been a surprise to him.

"In that?" said he exhibiting more amusement and scorn than I felt warranted.

"Yes," said I, and decided that was all I better say.

"Got any guns?" was the next query.

"Not a one," thinking that answer would release us from further custody.

"Well, wait," he ordered, as he started to walk away.

"You didn't tell us what's the matter," I shot after him.

"Oh, just a little murder," he threw back and kept on going.

We concluded we would do just as he said—so we waited.

As soon as he was well out of earshot, we talked freely among ourselves.

"But why on earth do you suppose they stop *us*? We haven't any firearms and they can see we're women." We had forgotten Mr. Miller! They surely couldn't suspect our good Samaritan!

The sand is heavy going in western Nebraska.

It was hot just sitting around. Perhaps the irritation and unhappiness over our needless detention may have made us somewhat more torrid under the collar than otherwise. But we waited. And we waited. And we waited.

We actually spent two hours waiting.

The man started toward us. Our spirits rose. He turned and went back to the group assembled and conferred a few moments. Then he came again in our direction. With not the slightest suggestion of a smile on his impassive face he said:

"All right. You can go."

"Thank you very much," I answered, "but would you tell us why you have held us all this time?"

He relaxed and became human long enough to confide that Raleigh Mann had been robbed and murdered in his cabin down in the "wash." That was all we could get out of him. Some time later we learned that a man and his wife were spending money rather lavishly in another town. The authorities, becoming suspicious that there might be some connection, brought near this couple Raleigh Mann's dog which had been injured during the murder. Without any hesitation the dog attacked the couple viciously. In that part of our country the law counts strongly on such evidence of guilt. The couple were given a trial but they paid for the crime. That was the sequel of the story for which we were held temporarily suspect.

The delay of two hours resulted in our getting no farther than Ogallala for that night. We were in a truly western atmosphere.[78]

Since we again raised our mileage, we looked hopefully forward to reaching Cheyenne on the morrow, foothills or no. At least we were no longer bogged down by *mud!* and as we continued to rise to higher elevation, we left behind us the heavy sand near the Platte River basin also.

We came to a tiny stream, alive with flowing water, and what looked like a small bridge for crossing.[79] But what a funny-looking bridge—it seemed

When you find a small bridge split in the middle, just ford *the stream!*

87

to have acquired a peak in the middle. This called for examination. Closer inspection showed it to have buckled and, while it *could* be crossed on *foot* it would not be easy to do with an automobile—for it didn't quite connect!

Just one thing to do here. So we do it! We look the stream over. It has a stony base and it's not too deep. We'll have to ford it. So, let's go! Hang on, everyone! We're going through! The method to use here is to edge up carefully—then make a run for it. Don't stop. Turning aside from the usual roadway, we choose a favorable path. Splash! Splash! The spray rushes up over the top of the radiator and we plow through, but we're on the other side before we know it. Back onto the road and on we go.

Undulating foothills of the Rockies, approaching Cheyenne, Wyoming.

After traversing so much barren country, we came upon a most unusual sight. To our left was a high bluff rising above us suddenly. The surprise of it was that it was covered from bottom to top with trees—and of all things, pine trees. This was close to the railroad again and as we approached the station we laughed at its name. That's right—it was Pine Bluff, the first railroad stop in Wyoming.[80]

From here on we saw huge ranches for sheep and cattle—as a matter of fact our highway ran directly through some of this privately-owned property. To keep the cattle in, there were gates we had to open and close behind us as we passed through. No matter how inconvenient it was, no one would think of neglecting this little chore in return for the right to pass. This part of the road was a mere trail from here into Cheyenne as it crossed the ranches and hills. But it was a beautiful ride, with ever-expanding views, as one looked across the rolling land to the distant horizon.

The main road traversed private cattle ranches. Gates must be opened and closed by all travelers.

Notes

66. This was three miles northwest of Denison.
67. The largest hotel in Denison, as listed in the 1915 *Complete Official Road Guide of the Lincoln Highway*, was Hotel Denison, $2 to $2.50 a night, with meals. It was located on the southeast corner of Broadway and 14th Streets, and razed

several years ago. The site is now occupied by a Ben Franklin store. Alice probably drove east to pick up 20th Street, Denison's only northbound through street, to drive to Sioux City.

68. The next few nights were spent at the West Hotel, between Third and Fourth on Nebraska Street. Razed in the 1970s, the site is now a parking lot.

69. The "Combination Bridge" was built in 1896 and replaced in 1981 by a new bridge, immediately upstream.

70. Alice's "little peanut of a hotel" was the Kennelly Hotel, on Court Street less than a block of the depot of the Chicago, St. Paul, Minneapolis, and Omaha Railroad. Built in 1898, it stood until 1923.

71. Most of Alice's route to Columbus probably has disappeared from the Nebraska state highway map.

72. Wisner's 2000 population was 1,253. It is on US 275. The Wisner Hotel was on the north side of Avenue E at Tenth Street. The two-story building, with seventeen rooms, was built in 1869, torn down in 1961.

73. The roads to Howells (pop. 615) are obvious from the current Nebraska highway map. It is on Nebr. 91.

74. The only hotel in Leigh in 1909 was the North-western, across Main Street and a half-block south of the present public library.

75. Alice probably would have turned due south on the Monastery Road just east of Creston (pop. 220) for a straight shot into Columbus, entering that town on present Eighteenth Street. She is back on the route of the future Lincoln Highway.

76. The North Platte River, which Alice now is following, rises in Jackson County, northern Colorado.

77. The bridge taken into North Platte is long gone. It was a block or two west of the present US 83 bridge.

78. Alice probably stayed in the Barrett Hotel on Spruce Street.

79. Probably Lodgepole Creek, which was followed to the west by the Pony Express in 1860, and the Lincoln Highway in 1913.

80. Alice probably entered Pine Bluffs over the route of present US 30, the Lincoln Highway. A large filling station, with more than a dozen gas pumps, straddled the state line, and now is a derelict. It was bypassed by I-80, less than a mile to the south.

9

Cheyenne to
Opal, Wyoming

CHEYENNE, WYOMING, in 1909 was a true frontier town, of larger population and dimension than the average. It was, nevertheless, a typical one with a conglomeration of Indians, cowboys and cattlemen on its streets; its stores, naturally, carrying supplies for this mixture of people and occupations. The buildings of frame construction and the dirt streets strongly resembled the sets we see nowadays for "Westerns" on TV. It did, however, boast one good hotel, The Inter-Ocean, which we enjoyed to the utmost before putting out across the southern part of the state for Salt Lake City.[81]

One of our special joys was the contact we had again with home as we picked up our more-than-welcome mail. Each one retired to read the latest news; to gather later and report on conditions at home. It was a great satisfaction to know that all were well and getting along fine—in spite of our absence! We didn't talk about how much we would like to see our dear ones. That might have been unwise, for tears were close to the surface. But just hearing from them made us light-hearted again as we pursued our journey westward.

Roads in Wyoming were scarcely what we would designate as such; they were wagon trails, pure and simple; at times, mere horse trails. Where the conveyances had usually been drawn by a team, there would be just the

Hermine standing in auto. This shows our equipment in the West.

two definite tracks—or maybe ruts—often grass-grown in between. On the other hand, where many one-horse rigs had passed, a third track would be visible in the middle through the grass or weeds. With no signboards and not too many telegraph poles, it was an easy matter to pick up a side trail and find oneself arrived at the wrong destination.

So the Cheyenne Maxwellites were insistent that we use pilot cars most of the way across the state. It took quite a bit of doing to get men qualified for the trip. Not too many were sufficiently experienced and not all of those were available. Finally, however, we enlisted the assistance of Mr. George Strawman and Mr. Armstrong to go from Cheyenne to Laramie, a distance of fifty miles, where they would be relieved by Will Goodale and Gus Schilling, who would continue with us to Rock Springs beyond the Continental Divide.

Between Cheyenne and Laramie there is relatively more traffic than west of the latter town. Considerable climbing is encountered, as there is

And how about this for the main road across the U.S.A.?

more or less constant ascent toward the summit of the Rockies near Rawlins. There were few towns, however, along this route and they were many miles apart—and not much when you got there!

After the completion of the building of the Union Pacific Railroad, a stone monument in the shape of an irregular pyramid was erected to commemorate the accomplishment of the Ames brothers. In 1869, in the face of strenuous opposition of people and conditions, these two determined men had brought this dream and heart-breaking work to a successful termination. In 1909 the roadway ran quite close to the monument; later a finer highway was built much farther away.[82] One must, then, leave the road to get a satisfactory view of the monument. What a pity, as it represents so great an achievement both scientifically and historically in the annals of our country.

While there were many grades and we were obliged to stop occasionally to cool the motor, thus affording the passengers the opportunity to chat and confer about the road ahead, the going was not too difficult, and we made the fifty miles for late lunch. The two pilots returned to Cheyenne, and Will Goodale and Gus Schilling took over for the stint to Rock Springs. "J.D." just got a transfer to the new pilot car and we followed on. From this point the trail was extremely indistinct and we would have had a bad time

Between Cheyene and Laramie, a stop to cool the engine and see the vast landscape.

without our leaders. At Rock River we found a fair-sized hotel near the railroad station.[83] For that matter, the whole town was by the railroad as it wasn't very big. There was rather surprisingly, I thought, a livery stable here and I was able to vary my usual ride by one on horseback in the early evening. When I mounted the little hill, outside the village, I saw on a neighboring rise a coyote yowling his bloodcurdling cry. There was no doubt I was truly in the West.

Anticipating the climb over the Divide, we left Rock Springs[84] at eight o'clock. Before long our Maxwell had a blow-out. We fixed that and went on.

After the earlier grades before Laramie, the land had stretched out into huge ranch country, some parts of which had fertile fields watered by irrigation ditches. They were crude water courses, across which our trail would pass from time to time, necessitating fording them. Naturally, to keep the water from escaping, they were constructed with a slight bank on each side of the ditch.

All hands man the block and tackle to pull the pilot car from the irrigation ditch.

Mr. Goodale's vehicle was in the lead, of course. All of a sudden I saw him turn slightly to the right to ford. Approaching, he went down deep with the front wheels, which in turn rapidly rose out of the water on the far side; the rear wheels followed the others quickly into the ditch. Whether the bank was steeper than he judged, I'll never know, or why he deviated from the trail, I can't imagine. The rear wheels now came to a complete stop, almost entirely under water, as millions of bubbles issued from his active exhaust. The motor never stopped but it wasn't doing him one bit of good at the moment. That automobile was really stuck!

Time for another conference! We had remained behind him but we got out and examined the conditions of the immediate predicament. It looked as if the bank were less deep where the trail had continued on its way through the ditch. We had a rope, a block and tackle, and plenty of people to man both, besides the drivers of the two autos. So we decided if I would cross the ditch at the shallower point and come around into the field facing the almost submerged pilot car, we could attach both the rope and the tackle and, with all people and both engines working together, we might yank him out. Our

The road follows a snake-like path near the railroad—our principal link with civilization across Wyoming.

Maxwell would be in reverse gear, with which we could obtain greater power and traction, while he could add the pull of his motor to help himself up the bank as much as possible. it was quite a layout when it was all ready for operation. With the throttle of both autos at the full, we made a mighty co-operating effort and practically hoisted him out.

This, then, was our second rescue of "the other fellow!"

That day we began to see new forms of scenery in the way of buttes and alkali lakes; lakes which have lured man and beast to the water's edge only to discover their mineral salts render the water unfit to drink. Each butte, an isolated hill or small mountain whose precipitous sides and flat or pointed tops, as the case may be, give it a curious and unique appearance, brought an unexpected variety in the landscape so barren in other respects. To our left, we saw also wonderful examples of eroded cliffs—huge hulks of

These eroded adobe cliffs were a novel bit of scenery to us.

land whose sides had been drained by the rains of centuries so that their present form resembled great folds like magnified pleatings in an enormous elephant's hide. This was all so amazing, so completely different from anything we had ever seen. Here and there, as we doubled back to the railroad, we would come across over-size snow-fences, almost never seen in the eastern parts of our country.

Many rivers, whose sources begin in the Rockies, have drained through this region producing extensive and frequently very deep arroyos washed out through the land. We came this day to one cut to a depth of probably sixty feet. There was a trail following down the side of this tremendous washout on the bias. We descended it with care and crossed the dry river bed to mount the opposite side. Going up was more difficult than going down, as the surface was gravelly and defied traction. It was far too narrow to do any sort of tacking so we had to negotiate it head on. Everyone out but the driver! Each passenger stood ready with rocks or blocks of wood to place under the rear wheels. The method was this: Give her the gas in low and pull ahead a few inches. Block the wheels. Repeat this process again and again. Eventually, with good power, stout and willing helpers, and plenty of time and patience, we reached the crest and were up on the plateau once more. This was a strenuous piece of work for all concerned and we were very proud of personnel and Maxwell, too. Incidentally, the girls had a week's exercise all at once!

Passing through the little village of Medicine Bow our thoughts reverted to the tale of Owen Wister, *The Virginian*, the locale of which novel was laid here. There were few buildings beside the railroad station, a general store and a saloon, so far as we could see.[85] Later we came to Ramsey, Wyoming, and gave it a little salute because of its name—no relation, however! We continued westward.

As we learned in Laramie, it would be necessary for us to obtain a permit to cross the railroad trestle of the Union Pacific near Ft. Steele. This was occasioned by the fact that the road bridge which formerly spanned the Platte River north of the trestle had been washed away during a flood and had not been replaced. The residents of Laramie showed little concern over this arrangement so we had anticipated it without too much dread. They had little reason to travel this piece of road except by wagon, when they may have forded the river. We were pretty unprepared for what this turned out to

Boy, what a climb out of this deep arroyo!

be!

But as we followed the trail in open—*very* open—country, we came to a place where the road crossed the railroad at the top of a small rise. Beyond this point there was no road. It just plain quit.

"Well, this looks like the place," said I.

"Sure does," someone added.

When they had said we must obtain permission to travel on the company's right of way from their station master, we supposed the station was at our end of the trip. Oh no, it was three-quarters of a mile away, beyond the trestle. The problem was to get a permit to do something we would have to do before we could get the permit! What a crazy world! We talked it over and agreed that all the others would proceed on foot to the station, walking the ties and the trestle. This was a single pair of rails at the top of an embankment twenty or more feet in height—not much ballast between the ties, and what there was was gravelly sand in which it was difficult to obtain foothold. Nice prospect confronting them if a train should arrive before they reached the station! Meanwhile I waited until they should obtain the permit and give me the high sign to come ahead. On and on they went and I hardly dared let my eyes drift away from them after they got near the other end. The last part was the trestle, open to the flowing water of the river below. No place for "scared cats."

Finally they arrived at the station and I watched and watched anxiously for the signal. Time was precious—for I must not miss the high sign, as the trip must be completed between scheduled trains in either direction. No place to go but up if anything faintly resembling a locomotive appeared.

There was no doubt much telegraphing back and forth on the part of the station master to receive clearance for our Maxwell to travel the right of way. It was an hour after they reached the station before that permission was received. Finally I saw the wave. All aboard for the perilous journey!

The crossing was at grade, even though the rails were on the elevated embankment, as I mentioned before; so it was not too difficult to get the vehicle in position. The wheels on the left side of the auto must travel in between the two rails, the ones on the right on the outside of the righthand rail, between it and the edge of the bank. This, being of sandy surface, had to be carefully negotiated. One could easily get too close to the edge and slip over the brink and down the bank. Remember too, that there was practically no ballast, and the design the Maxwell must travel was like a Greek fret. All right. Here we go! Feed a little gas! Let in the clutch!

BUMP!

Touch the brake, so the bump isn't so great it throws you out of rhythm. Repeat the process.

BUMP!

BUMP!

BUMP! Three-quarters of a mile of this, one bump at a time. There are more bumps in that distance than you would imagine. As if living one day at a time in periods of stress, I lived one bump at a time. Each bump was a mark of progress and I had to keep going. What a spot this would be for another broken axle! The ties were just the correct distance apart so they might hold the wheels as in a cradle and prevent moving ahead, unless the auto was kept in motion.

Just ahead lay the trestle. No doubt the girls were more anxious about my crossing it than they had been regarding their own. Each of us had a contribution to make in the solution of this problem—and made it without question. This was *my* turn. It was one of those places where you don't look down—you keep plowing steadily on.

The Platte River was a pretty stream, I saw *after* I had reached the station. Up until that moment I had had "other fish to fry!" so scenery never entered my mind as I bumped my way over this last hurdle. The thing which really concerned me seriously, though, was the sharp pain which had intensified as the journey neared its end. It was excruciating. I was convinced I had acute appendicitis! However, as I rested a while, it proved to be a severe case of *jolt*-itis, from which I recovered shortly. And, fortunately, the two axles, which had replaced the broken ones enroute, must have been of sterner stuff than the originals.[86]

From the station, our road took over once more and we proceeded to the crossing of the Continental Divide. No matter what its surface, this trail must have seemed heaven to us for the remainder of that day. Could anything more happen? We hoped not, but there were still many miles and some rough spots to come. Arriving at Rawlins, we found we had made but 81 miles for the day; but considering all the misfortunes, perhaps that was not too bad.[87]

The following day's drive was over a very bad road between Bitter Creek and Rock Springs with a blow-out to give us variety; then a storm at the end of the day, from which we *almost* escaped, leaving us not too wet. After Rawlins, Mr. Miller and our two pilots left us, and we took on a local pilot to Evanston.

A light rain delayed us in take-off until ten. We had no sooner left town than we had another blow-out. Riding the ties is pretty tough on fabric tires and no doubt they were now registering *their* indignation against what they had been obliged to endure.

It is difficult to give one, living in the present perfection of roads and signposts, a true idea of how completely lacking these were in most of the western states. The well-known Automobile *Blue Books* were issued in sections for states east of the Mississippi River; but west of that waterway there was a great gap of information. Many a time we found our correct route by following poles which carried the greater number of wires. Most of the time we were right, yet there were occasions when we chose the wrong direction and were obliged to retrace our way to the intersection and try again.

I have spoken several times of our pilot car. The road situation was the reason for taking the precaution of having such a leader. It was his job to show us the correct trail in this uncharted land. "J.D." would often ride with the pilot instead of taking the train; this gave diversity to his job and saved the company the train fare! Once or twice his presence also supplied an extra pair of hands to help us out of difficulties or to get the pilot car out of a ditch! And don't forget, he *was* my "percheron" on one notable occasion!

It struck us that possibly our new pilot was not too familiar with the trail we were following. We seemed to be taking the route of a Reo which preceded us. This brought us to the entrance of a mine! Another attempt introduced us to a sandpit. Still another try and we came up behind the same Reo waiting for an Oregon Short Line train to shift at a crossing. We also saw a number of those deep arroyos but were able to get out in good shape.

After running up mileage again in the 80's we stopped for the night at Opal, Wyoming. The name sounded rather intriguing and we looked forward to this little "gem."[88]

So far, in all our travels, hotels in small places were rather "sketchy" in accommodations, but rooms and beds had been clean. Of course, we were still a long traveling era away from twin beds and Beautyrest mattresses. But, considering the location and the lack of abundant facilities, lodgings were acceptable and we did not complain.

But the hotel at Opal was an outstanding exception.

Hermine and I shared the same room always and, of necessity, the same bed. We were both good sleepers, however, so we managed all right.

When we stopped driving at Opal it was still daylight and there was someone at the entrance of the hotel to show us to our rooms on the second floor. There is no notation in my diary as to our dinner, but the *night* still remains vivid! Since we liked to start in good time in the mornings, we retired early.

I had been asleep for hours when I was aroused by Hermine's moving about considerably. As the disturbance continued, I said, "What's the matter with you?" If she had been a light sleeper she probably would have been more aware of the situation. When she answered sleepily, "I don't know. I seem to itch all over," that was all I needed to hear. I bounded up quickly, lighted the oil lamp and took one look at the bed. One look was enough! Immediately I began hurriedly to dress, and Hermine, now half awake, inquired, "What are you going to do?" I parried with, "I don't know, but I'm going to get out of *here*, that's for sure."

That must have sounded like a rather unsatisfactory reply, for where *could* we go in this section of the country at this hour of the night? The time was 2 a.m. as we made our way quietly down the stairs into the so-called office. Not a soul was around. The night clerk, at this hour, was a *blackboard* hanging on the wall upon which was scribbled the numbers of the unoccupied rooms! When a traveler came seeking a place to sleep (and it was likely to be a sheepherder) he consulted the board for information and proceeded to his "downy." One could only hope his eyesight was good and that he read numbers correctly! All keys to the rooms had long ago been lost!

In the office there were several chairs and a circular table. That solved our need for the time being. We sat down, laid our heads on the hard table and resumed our night's rest (?). In the morning when the hotel began to stir and the help—or maybe the owners—came in, it was significant that no one asked why we were there. Was it a frequent happening? we wondered. The girls had luckily escaped. Apparently the pests had chosen *our* room as more desirable for their convention than the one next door. In justice to other places, it is only fair to tell you this was the only occurrence of the kind—but one was more than sufficient.

The town's name *Opal*, was assuredly a misnomer—no jewel, to us!

Notes

81. Chances are the road from Pine Bluffs to Cheyenne was a straight-shoot two-track to Egbert. It probably followed section lines up to Burns, Hillsdale, Durham, and Archer, before entering Cheyenne on Pershing, then slanting southwest to 16th Street, later Lincolnway. Alice probably marveled at the magnificent Union Pacific depot, which they passed before stopping for the night at the Inter-Ocean Hotel. Located on the northwest corner of West Lincolnway and Capitol Avenue, it was one block west of the site of the future Plains Hotel. The Inter-Ocean burned not long after Alice arrived, killing six people, and the site is now occupied by the Hynds Building, vacant for many years. The historic buildings just to the east went up in flames in December 2004. As Alice drove west of Cheyenne she passed the hamlet of Granite Canyon, source of the Sherman granite used as ballast for the Union Pacific railroad and many of Wyoming's gravel roads.

82. The Maxwell took the old way to Laramie, not Telephone Canyon, which would not be put through for another decade. Alice would have followed the 1901 route of the Union Pacific to pass by Ames Monument. Oliver and Oakes Ames were financial backers of the Union Pacific. The "finer highway" is today's I-80, formerly US 30, about a mile south of the dirt two-track at the monument.

83. The adventurers would have had to pass through the village of Laramie on the way to Rock River.

84. Alice meant to write "Rock River," not "Rock Springs."

85. About 20 miles west of Rock River, Medicine Bow currently sports The Virginian hotel, opened just two years after Alice passed through. She would have turned south at the site of the future hotel to cross the UP tracks, then west to follow the railroad grade to Fort Steele.

86. Alice's route to Fort Steele was over the future Lincoln Highway, which coursed about two miles north of I-80. The fort itself, 1868-86, was built on the north side of the railroad to protect the tracks from Indian predations. The fort is now a state historic site.

87. Alice actually crossed the Continental Divide twice. Like many motorists, and in fact the state itself in those days, there was much confusion on its location, due partially because of the Continental Divide Basin. The first crossing is actually about a dozen miles west of Rawlins, not east. The other rim is crossed about twenty miles west of Wamsutter.

88. Curiously, Alice made no mention of the stunning geology along the Green River. She was traveling the route of both the future Lincoln Highway and the later US 30. She left the route of the Lincoln near Granger, when she turned northwest to follow later US 30. Opal, with a current population of 101, is fifteen miles east

of Kemmerer. The Opal Hotel, built in 1902, burned in 1927. The top floor of the Opal Mercantile served as a hotel at a later time, and a ghost sign is still on the wall of the brick building. The town was founded in 1881 when the Oregon Short Line railroad came through.

10

Opal to Reno, Nevada

WHEN THE girls appeared for breakfast, their eyes grew large with surprise to see us already down with bags and all. Our conversation during the meal was of the hushed variety; but we were able to impart the main facts of our night's woeful experience and discover, in return, that our pals were unscathed. Our main object was to leave this town of the gem-like appellation with all speed.

As we filled the Maxwell with gasoline and oil a lovely new Pierce-Arrow drove up with three men aboard. There were so few long-distance travelers by motor in 1909 that the common interest served as a perfectly proper introduction and we compared road information. They, too, were headed westward. The youngest of the group, Lynn Thompson, had just been graduated from Yale University. His father, former Mayor Ezra Thompson, Tom Botterill, and Lynn, all of Salt Lake City, were enroute home with this new motorcar from the factory at Buffalo, New York. It seemed wise to drive along together.

The way to go, they said, was via Oakley north to Kemmerer, then turn south to Evanston. We started and they followed as far as Oakley. Then they took the lead to Evanston where we stopped for lunch and fuel. When Mayor Thompson concluded he would press on homeward, and invited us to

The Thompson party driving their new Pierce-Arrow from the factory in Buffalo, New York, to their home in Salt Lake City.

tag along, we were all for it. Since our pilot from Rock Springs was to leave us after lunch, it was wonderful to have someone who was familiar with the area whom we could follow into the Mormon capital. Lynn's sister, Norinne, had been in Ogden, and after we passed through Weber and Echo Canyons, we were to wait at an intermediate town while they made the little side trip to get her.

The sun was getting low but there was still enough light to see the sights and even to take photographs as we drove through these massive wooded mountains. We liked the change from the barren scenery of Wyoming. One side of the pass would be bathed in brilliant sunlight while heavy shadows engulfed the opposite side, making the scene appear almost

107

black-and-white in dazzling contrast.

We had heard Devil's Slide mentioned, and were curious to see it, but were quite unprepared for its appearance. Beside our road was a mountain. Descending its steep side were two vertical parallel ridges of solid stone ten or twelve feet high and not too many feet apart. The declivity was terrific. It would have made more of a *drop* than a *slide* for the aforementioned Devil, I should judge. No Devil was apparent at the time we saw it! I believe I should have felt a bit sorry for him if he had had to slide down it. Quite a sight! So all-by-itself, and so stupendous.[89]

The road winds back and forth through these deep canyons in its approach to Salt Lake City. Finally we reached the handsome capital with its wide, clean streets, all nestled so beautifully at the west slope of the Wasatch Range. Northwest of the city lay the Great Salt Lake, and to the southwest, the Great Salt Lake Desert which we had to cross later.

Salt Lake City was one of the most important milestones in our trip. We would get mail; we would have the Maxwell gone over and put in shape for what might be the hardest part of its journey, so far as climbing and heat were considered. And we would pick up our Maxwell pilot, Mr. Sam Sharman, state representative for the company, who would escort us in his little two-cylinder roadster all the way to Reno. There was also much of interest to be seen. Altogether, we thought we would stay several days. And we did.

The whole Thompson family were wonderful hosts and saw to it that we were shown the sights of their city and its environs. There was the impressive Mormon Temple (which we were not Mormon enough to enter), and the Tabernacle, that acoustical jewel of interesting and unique structure, erected without nails. *There* can be heard most satisfying concerts of beautiful artistry exquisitely rendered. It was a real treat to our ears starved for some first-class music for a long period of time.

And the mail! That was one of our greatest treats. A few of our most skeptical friends told us after our return that they didn't feel any too sure we would actually get that far, but they would take a chance, for they knew if we did arrive we would really be anxious to hear from as many as possible. We reveled in the size of the pouch we found awaiting us. It gave us all that happy touch with our families which makes it possible to keep going a little longer.

Our spring bumpers and shock absorbers were in poor condition after crossing over the railroad ties so we delayed a day for repairs, taking the precaution to have the spring leaves separated and oiled and then wrapped for protection on the desert and mountain roads ahead. Also, I borrowed from Mr. Botterill tools to scrape the cylinder heads while other things were being done. We spent three days there in all, and were able to tuck in a visit to Saltair on the Lake and had a swim in that fantastically buoyant water where it is hard to keep a man down.[90]

By the time appointed for our departure on Saturday morning, we had added another carload to our Maxwell and Mr. Sharman's tiny roadster. Mr. Joe Richards, his teen-age nephew Jack, and Mr. Frank Irving were to accompany us in Mr. Richard's Pierce through the most formidable part of the Utah desert.

We left Salt Lake City reluctantly, bidding farewell to the generous Thompsons, and drove along the southern shore of the Salt Lake past Garfield and some mining company headquarters to Grantsville, where we lunched. From there the road turns southward through extremely barren country. One

Frank Irving, Jack Richards, Mrs. Powell, Mrs. Atwood, Sam Sharman, Joe Richards, Miss Jahns at Grantsville, Utah.

109

sees nothing but arid land, many prairie dog holes and occasionally one of the fat tawny little animals sitting atop his residence looking inquiringly about.

If I wanted to take a picture of one—he darted with the speed of light down into his burrow. My desire was kindled and I lay face down on the ground, waiting for him to reappear, only to have him emerge via another hole and yes, almost grin at me in triumph! I had to give it up as an im*prob*ability, if not an im*poss*ibility.

We ran along for miles on the squirmy trail, just two packed tracks for our wheels, curving around through the sagebrush. Suddenly we felt a tremendous bump at the front and immediately the entire front end and radiator were aimed at an angle toward the ground. I got out to look things over. It was an awful-looking sight to behold! The front wheels were spread

Prairie dogs may be almost extinct now, but in 1909 they dug their front door right in the track of our wheels—with this result.

wide apart as if they never wanted to have anything to do with each other and certainly had no intention of working in harmony again. It all happened because a prairie dog had chosen to build his front door right in the wagon tracks we were traveling. There was no other path to take; so when the wheel hit this yawning hole the bolt came out of the tie rod connecting the wheels and—there we were! In the accident, the spring seat had broken away from the axle. What to do?

Frank Irving knew there was a forge at Orr's Ranch, a few miles ahead. We took out our roll of wire carried as a precautionary supply for emergency, and did the best we could to wind it tightly around the spring and axle until we reached Orr's Ranch, driving with utmost care and little speed. On arrival, Frank heated a piece of strip steel and, removing the wire, bound the heated strip around the axle and spring in its place. Under normal conditions this would have been sufficient.[91] But in this wild and unpredictable country one never knew what lay ahead!

This event had caused us considerable delay; but our friends were still determined we must cross that bad desert stretch, so we drove on. Having left Salt Lake City at ten in the morning Saturday, we kept on until three o'clock Sunday morning when they suggested we might take a respite. I was dead tired. I "descended" from the auto and practically sank to the ground—not, however, before some kindly member of the party had considerately grabbed the back seat cushion from our Maxwell and shoved it under me for a bed. I went off to sleep so rapidly I never knew who did it or how the others were provided for.

At 6 a.m. (only *three* hours later) we were roused to start on again. Ordinarily I like an eight-hour rest, so I was very, very short of my quota that night. Not too much later we pulled up at Fish Springs, a tiny settlement. I recall seeing only one building, a long adobe structure, but they said we could eat. We were not *too* particular *what* it was. I was not a coffee drinker at that period of my life, so when the man announced he had only dry cereal, canned tomatoes and coffee, I'm sure I shuddered. Maybe the others shuddered too at the dry cereal! But it was a general store and not a restaurant, so the poor man was doing the best he could. We did not even ask to supplement it with the usual bread-and-butter and sugar. Frankly, I believe it is good for us *not* to be able to get just what we want sometimes; but to be obliged to accept what is at hand, make the best of it and, in addition, be

Breakfast stop at Fish Springs, Utah—corn flakes, canned toma-toes, and coffee, which I didn't drink then!

thankful. And that was certainly one of those times![92]

We pressed on. Arriving at Callao after noon, we stopped for dinner at a large building where they served us on the second floor. While we were enjoying the excellent meal, we noticed a funeral procession filing down the main street, and thought how forlorn a spot to lay away a dear one.

The restfulness of relaxing at dinner came to an end and we put out again, hoping to reach Ely, or at least Ibapah, a tiny hamlet close to the Nevada border. Above the mountains in the northwest, which we were about to cross, hung a dark cloud, from the under side of which, like moss draped from the trees of the South, was the unmistakable evidence of a cloudburst coming our way. One gets in the habit of watching for this sort of formation in sections of the Far West and keeping one's eyes on the direction of its travel. We never actually got any of the rain from that cloud—but we *did* have to deal with the results of it.

There was a long up-grade pull and as we went along we first saw a tiny stream running at the right side of the road. Our trail wound and climbed and the rivulet temporarily dropped out of sight, only to appear much more lusty in size and with stronger current in the flow. The girls began to show some uneasiness, but there was no use borrowing trouble until we came to it. It still kept to the side of the road and caused us no inconvenience.

When we next returned to the route of the descending water, we just *had* to change plans—and quickly! Right ahead of us instead of the road, lay a gaping hole—fully 12 feet broad and three to four feet deep, still partially filled with swiftly flowing water. Each vehicle had come to a sudden stop, the occupants gazing with open-eyed consternation at the problem confronting us. Under ordinary conditions it would have posed a difficult question, but, with our auto disabled at the front, we had a particularly hard nut to crack.

It is an honor to report that no one ever suggested quitting or showed any attitude other than the desire to attack the formidable situation and conquer it. They knew my intention of driving the automobile from one coast to the other so they refrained from even asking at any point of the journey if they might take the wheel. It wouldn't have been accepted either, short of my breaking an arm or a leg!

There were the three cars: the little light roadster of Mr. Sharman, the heavy Pierce of Mr. Richards, and ours of medium weight. As we chatted about the way to proceed, Mr. Sharman said:

"I believe it will be best for me to tackle the crossing first. Then if the Pierce will follow, the extra weight of it will tear down the sides of the bank enough to make the climb down and up simpler for the disabled Maxwell." That seemed to all the soundest reasoning.

So the little Maxwell started, eased itself carefully down the very steep, almost vertical side, through the water and up the other side. The men joined to help it up the bank with all the push they had. The brave little red roadster plowed ahead at full throttle and up she went. Cheers on all sides!

Then came the Pierce. As it started down the near bank it pulled with it a great quantity of dirt from the side, thus lowering the slope for us. The far bank, already partially broken, was a good hard pull but the Pierce had plenty of power and up she went, too. More cheers from the anxious gallery!

And now it was our turn! To lighten the auto, everyone was already out but me. I started to inch it gently as possible down the bank, just a tiny distance at a time. The pressure against the front wheels was tremendous, as the auto was tipped at an angle of forty or more degrees and it was all I could do to remain upright on the seat. Going down was ticklish, but things held until the front wheels rested on the bottom of the stream still flowing madly. Then, as I attempted to lower the rear wheels to the level in preparation for climbing the opposite side, the axle rolled under the body of the auto, and the front end pitched forward as at the prairie dog hole.

The day following the prairie dog encounter we had to negotiate this gully twelve feet across and four feet deep washed out of the main road by a sudden cloudburst.

At this point Frank Irving took off his shoes, rolled up his trousers and waded into the water to jack up the front end. He patiently attached the axle and spring with the strip of steel. We repeated the performance only to have it happen again. This went on with several repetitions, all of which consumed a lot of time as well as patient forbearance—mostly on the part of Frank Irving, I should say. Time was running along much too fast and before we finished one of the party said, "Hadn't we better send an auto ahead to get accommodations for the night?"

That sounded like a first class idea, so the Pierce went on with the men who were the least necessary for the job at hand. And we went on jacking and going a few inches—plunging—jacking—and a few inches more. Finally we were at the point where we started to climb to the other side. This went better than going down, as some of the weight of the auto itself was held back from the front end. Just as we were about to attain the summit on the far side the Pierce returned to our group.

Amazed to have them come back, Frank Irving said, "What did you come back for?"

The reply was a definitely depressing one. "Well," said Mr. Richards, "if you think this is bad, you ought to see the one six miles from here!" And he proceeded to describe its size.

Well—now that we had all crossed this frightful chasm, it looked seriously as if it were of no avail. We would have to go back to Callao for the night. So, back across the washout came the little Maxwell roadster and the Pierce. It was thought best to leave the transcontinental auto in its weakened condition perched up on the far side of the washout and to return to it later. So we emptied it of its contents, human and otherwise, crowded into the other two autos, and went back down the mountain to Callao. The people there were as surprised to see us as our crowd had been to have the Pierce return with its bad news. But Callao could take care of us overnight. We buzzed and buzzed with conversation during the rest of the evening and came to some agreement as to our next move.

The Salt Lake City people, except Mr. Sharman, were to return to the capital in the morning and would order a new front axle from San Francisco. It must be shipped by train and the nearest station was 90 miles away. That meant it would need to be trucked over the road to Callao and the earliest it could arrive would be by the Thursday noon stage. There was absolutely nothing to do in this tiny burg, so the girls decided they would take the stage to Ibapah and go on to Ely and await us there. Poor outlook for Mr. Sharman and me, but it was our job, so we took it on the chin. Things looked pretty bleak after everyone departed.[93]

Fortune smiled on us in one special way, however, for we discovered next day that there was a blacksmith in this little town—and a good one, too. He said he could forge another spring seat on the original axle if he had that one in hand. Why didn't someone tell us that before the others left? Well, on Monday Mr. Sharman and I went back to the scene of our temporary debacle and pulled that axle out of the Maxwell and brought it back to the smith. He worked all day Tuesday and finished it late Wednesday afternoon. It was so close to the time for the new one to come that we thought we should wait until the time for its arrival.

About 11 a.m. on the morrow the truck and team rolled into town and we watched anxiously while mail and packages were unloaded. Nothing faintly resembling an axle came forth! So with our renovated one we bade farewell a second time to Callao and returned in the roadster to our vehicle on the mountain, blessing the local blacksmith for his ability. It took the two of us until 5 that evening to replace it; and we took off in the two autos, reaching Ibapah for the night.[94] The woman who ran the little inn asked, much to our surprise and embarrassment: "Do you want one room?" We hastened to explain that, while we were both married, it was not to each other, and we would have to have two! This amusing incident closed the washout matter with a smile and so eased the tension of a bad situation of several days' duration.

The state of Nevada is almost completely made up of north-south mountain ranges partitioned from each other by long narrow valleys in which there is little population and less vegetation; the roads were mere trails and difficult to follow. Next morning when we left Ibapah, anxious to get to Ely and pick up the girls, we crossed the first range and came to a fork in the road. Since Ely lay off to our left, we naturally thought the left fork would lead us to our goal. No house to stop and ask, and no signpost—also at this point no wires to follow. We chose the left fork but after we had continued for a few miles and seemed to be getting nowhere, it dawned on me something was wrong so we stopped and held a council. I knew there was a pass we must cross as Ely lay in another valley, but there was none in sight. We had secured some maps from the Clason Map Company in Denver and there was a chance the girls might have left them under the rear seat. Up with the cushion—there they were! It took a while to find the correct section in the right state, as they were very detailed maps occupying many separate sheets. At last we found it. Yes, *there* was the fork in the road, and sure enough it was the *right* one which led up over Schellbourne Pass into the Steptoe Valley to Ely.[95]

We retraced the miles to the place where the trail divided and took the other fork. At least we could now proceed with a feeling of certainty. The trail looked misleading at first at it went straight toward the north. But before long it bent around to the west, ascended the long grade up the pass and there before us lay the Steptoe Valley. The road improved, we skimmed along and were soon united with our companions.

The girls gave us a truly rousing welcome. Were we glad to see them![96]

Their stay in Ely had been a pleasant change, for it was an active town. Nettie had always been an ardent sports fan and she was all agog because "Tex" Rickard, the prominent fight promoter, was staying at the hotel at the time. She had had a chance to meet him personally and have some chats with him—so she was aglow with the excitement of her experience.

During the early evening we took a short walk around the town. The girls had pleasure in showing us the various places of interest they had seen.

"See! That's the Chinese laundry where we had some of our clothes washed—and ironed, for a change. They look very nice."

I glanced in the window as we passed. Charlie was still ironing. He never observed union hours. He just kept on until he was caught up in his work, no matter when. Recognizing the girls as recent customers, he gave a smiling nod and went on with his job. All at once I saw he was preparing to sprinkle a batch of clothes. So I said, "Let's watch him a minute."

We all stopped and looked. Yes, Charlie was sprinkling, all right. I had my doubts whether they had ever seen a Chinese laundryman sprinkle things in his own inimitable fashion. Fascinated, they stood rooted to the spot as Charlie imbibed a quarter of a glassful of water and immediately sprayed it out again in a fine mist over the garments to be ironed. You never saw more surprised expressions. Hermine remarked, "Well, if I'd known that before, I don't think I would have had my clothes done there. I've a good mind to wash them over."

"Oh, no," replied Maggie, "don't do that. I know how you feel but if you hadn't seen it you wouldn't suspect. Think of all the people wearing clothes that have been done that way—and don't know it!"

"Yes, but look at all the germs he may be spreading! It's so unsanitary. I'm not so good at that 'mind over matter' stuff," replied Hermine.

"I'm not either," retorted Maggie, "but I'm not going to wash all those things again myself. I'll just try to forget what I saw."

Nettie had taken no part in this conversation but strolled on down the street without comment. But next morning Maggie let it slip that Nettie had rinsed out the nightdress that Charlie had ironed for her!

We were all "rarin' to go" so we did not linger in Ely more than that night. Nevada was going to be quite a challenge in the way of roads, we learned. It would be tough, no doubt. The state was the 7th in area—think what that means—and the population of the *entire state* was around 80,000, less than a small city, and 48th in the nation! There was no natural material to assist in the building of roads. Yet in minerals it was one of the richest states. They erected hotels for the miners long before they made decent highways.

There was some message Mr. Sharman had to receive before we could leave Ely, so I cleaned up the Maxwell while we waited. An old Montana friend of Mr. Sharman's, Bert Fuller, who ran a café in town, made us a delicious lunch. When at last we were ready to depart in the early afternoon, the Mayor and a group of mining folk were on hand to see us off and wish us the best of luck with a regular Indian war whoop as a salute. That was a novelty! We hadn't had one of those before! But the unexpectedness and sincerity of it sent us off in good spirits and laughing.

It wasn't that we had so many miles to go to Eureka, but it was up and down and around. We had some trouble with the carburetor in this altitude but only once were bothered with radiator overheating. We were traveling south and I thought the motor seemed to be getting pretty hot. We weren't climbing and there appeared to be no reason for it. Finally I figured it out—the wind was behind us and was neutralizing the action of the fan by creating a vacuum. Fortunately, we had taken the precaution to purchase a South African water bag. This is a simple but wonderful contraption, consisting of an envelope of heavy canvas perhaps 10 by 16 inches in size; in one upper corner is a large cork attached by a cord, so the stopper will not be lost, and across the top of the bag is a stout handle of twine. When this bottle is filled with water and suspended from a handy knob or projection on the automobile, the gradual seepage of the moisture through the canvas cools the contents by its evaporation. These are in common use in desert sections of our country to this day, but they were new to us. It is an easy way to provide cool drinking water as well as refills for the radiator in transit. With this we were able to replenish the water and continue.

Some of the climbs were so taxing we were obliged to fill our radiator from a roadside water trough.

When the road surface was good enough to permit the driver to relax a bit, we had quite a conversation on the subject of animal life along the way. "Don't you think it's strange we have not seen more animals during our travels through this wild country?" asked Hermine. "I've been watching for them every day but outside of the Shetland ponies and the little pigs in Iowa I don't recall many others. With all the ranches we passed I should think we would find more horses and cattle."

There did seem to be a scarcity of live animals. We had gone through so many ranch gates to keep the cattle in, but had seen little evidence of the actual presence of livestock, though I had noticed a few bleached carcasses of cattle that had died—nothing left but the head and horns!

"Remember I saw a coyote when I went horseback in Wyoming." The others had not been with me at the time, so they missed that one. "And I saw two rattlers coiled up in the sun by the roadside," I added. At this the girls shuddered. Safe within the auto then, the driver was very brave!

"As a matter of fact, I think there have been mighty few birds, too," said Maggie. Perhaps in desert regions we did not look for many as there was so little water for them to drink. We saw huge magpies in their striking black-and-white plumage and some rather small birds of nondescript shade, blending with the desert soil so as to be well-nigh invisible, and flying madly about in the manner of flycatchers.

"I have seen a few horned toads," I remarked.

"Why didn't you tell us?" they chimed together.

"They are so hard to see when they crouch close to the ground and I wasn't sure until we were past them," I answered. "I'll try and point one out to you."

In a moment I spied one and said: "Look there, beyond that clump of sagebrush." I slowed down to give them a view of the jagged-shaped object. He was watching us keenly, on the alert for this huge monster in his vicinity. His throat puffed back and forth in his excitement but he never moved from the spot. He was difficult to discern but obligingly kept quiet. Our departure must have relieved him.

In and out we wove, around small hills and occasionally through an arroyo, neither deep nor large in this section. We couldn't see our road very far in advance, however, because of the type of terrain.

Maggie started to ask, "Do you think that cloud over there looks like a thun—"

She stopped suddenly and the question remained unfinished.

Curiosity made us all look around us. Over to the right rode a dozen

Indians on horseback. They were dressed in trousers but were bare from the waist up. That wasn't so strange—but what was, was that they were all carrying *drawn* bows and arrows! The sagebrush grew so high that we could not see below the knees of the men. It was, to us, a most unusual sight but we had no idea of fear—at least—I hadn't at the time. They were riding parallel to our route and it seemed fitting to have such an accompaniment in this kind of country. It was rather enjoyable.

Suddenly, like a trained phalanx in an army, the entire group wheeled to the left and appeared to be coming directly at us! I could almost feel the color drain from my face. I had read—not too long ago—about Indians having attacked people in the western United States. Dreadful thoughts raced through my terrified mind faster than I can tell it. Nothing to do but *appear* unafraid and keep right on going.

As they drew nearer to our roadway, I realized they were a trifle in advance of us. I wondered if they intended to cut us off and stop us. By now they were so hot on the hunt that they were letting out regular war whoops from time to time.

Suddenly across the roadway ahead leapt a jackrabbit, bent madly on escape from his wild pursuers. The Indians never slowed down nor paid the least attention to us. They no doubt captured their unfortunate quarry, with all those skilled archers on his tail. For our part, we gave forth one glorious sigh of relief, when we discovered the object of their hunt was a poor desert animal instead of four eastern females! The love of life was *very* strong in all of us that afternoon, and I trust our lack of consideration for the rabbit may be forgiven.

Several times that day we had trouble finding our way—and no one around to ask! We were delayed by that considerably. Finally a puncture caused by a nail brought our arrival at Eureka to 11 p.m.[97]

Each day was a succession of more climbs, more difficulty getting on the right road, sometimes a blow-out and plenty of rough going. But we all enjoyed our overnight stay at Pat Walsh's ranch west of Austin. The ranch house wasn't always occupied, but we were lucky to find someone there who took us in hospitably. Come breakfast time, we had quite a surprise. The door from the kitchen opened and waddling in to the dining room was a giant-size, fat Indian squaw bearing for our start-the-day meal—No, you'd never guess it—of all things—lamb chops and chocolate cake! As one we gasped. Did I say we had to take things as they were? Well, we did. Willy, nilly, we all ate lamb chops and chocolate cake for breakfast. I'm sure it was the first time, and I rather believe it will be the last—by choice.

We made an early start after this breakfast, anyway—off at 5:30 a.m. In spite of the time of departure we consumed additional time getting on the wrong road and having to retrace our tracks. We had been told it was an advantage to let some of the air out of our tires when traveling in heavy sand, but doing so tore out one of the tire valve stems and gave us more trouble.

In the midst of all this hard going we found a man walking alone on the desert. Mr. Sharman gave him a lift in his roadster to Rawhide where we stopped. This place had been a very active mining town but was rather running down even when we were there. To us it was a roost for the night, however. We looked forward to being in Reno the next evening.[98]

In Rawhide, Nevada, one buys oil at the general store.

Leaving Rawhide there was an 8-mile climb followed by a 7-mile coast. Nice traveling while it lasted! The desert was hot and some parts of the road had very high centers. Fortunate we were that the Maxwell's differential stood many inches above the ground to allow for liberal clearance. We began to see beautiful ranches again, watered by irrigation from reservoirs in that fertile valley. At Fallon, Mr. Sharman had to repair tubes before he went on—and he badly needed a shave! He just wasn't going into Reno looking like a miner!

On through Hazen, Fernley and Wadsworth the road was pretty fair; but the image which is most vivid in my mind was the unexpected view as we drove over the mountain in the late evening and looked upon the little city of Sparks. I think I shall never forget the surprise of that vista bursting upon us in the darkness. Here was a hollow in which lay a community brilliantly lighted with electricity! Right off the dark and barren desert, this almost bowled us over. It was situated only a couple of miles from Reno and was connected to it—by trolley! Surprise! Surprise! Suddenly we had returned to civilization![99]

It was close to midnight when we drew up at the Riverside Hotel in Reno, but the greetings of the San Francisco and Sacramento Maxwellites, on hand to lead us on our final lap to the Golden Gate, could be heard above the rushing waters of the Truckee River flowing by the side of the building. And our spirits, in spite of the hour and our long day, were happy and bright as the dawn.[100]

Notes

89. While Alice crossed the Bear River to enter Evanston on the route of the later Lincoln Highway, her route in the city was entirely different. She did enter Utah on the same gravel road, and her path in Echo Canyon probably would have been the same road taken by the Lincoln Highway, with few exceptions. This road is now a fine asphalt road just north of I-80 and the Union Pacific Railroad. She would have followed the 1913 Lincoln Highway through the town of Echo and down Weber River Canyon across the river from present I-84. Devil's Slide is about eight miles west of Echo, and there is a turnout off the west-bound lanes, immediately opposite Devil's Slide.

90. Alice probably drove on north on or near the route of present I-84, turning left

just south of Ogden to arrive in Salt Lake City. There have been three of the Moorish-looking Saltair Resorts, some twelve miles west of the city. The first, visited by Alice and her companions, was sixteen years old in 1909. It burned to the ground in 1924. A replacement burned in the 1970s and the current version has a large dance floor, museum, concessions, and a gift shop.

91. Alice would have turned left, away from the lake shore, and followed the Skull Valley Road south to Orr's Ranch. The ranch still stands, and still thrives. The log building next to where Frank would have heated the steel still stands as well. The ranch is the home of Dennis and Shirley Orr Andrus. Shirley is the granddaughter of one of the Orr brothers, who would have welcomed the visitors, as Dennis and Shirley do today.

92. The proprietor was John J. Thomas, who moved into the Fish Springs Pony Express station shortly after the turn of the century. By the time Alice arrived he was living in the adjacent Overland Stage station, and after the Lincoln Highway passed his ranch he did a booming business hauling tourists out of the bogs along the highway. Nothing remains of the ranch buildings, and Fish Springs is now a National Wildlife Refuge.

93. We can find no evidence of a hotel in Callao. Alice and her companion probably lodged in one of the few homes in the village.

94. Alice probably spent the night at the Sheridan Ranch. Owen Sheridan's "hotel," although still standing, was not built until Lincoln Highway traffic picked up, in the middle 'teens. The current occupants are hay bales.

95. Alice made no mention of the Tippett Ranch, about fifteen miles west of the Utah line, but it was a going concern in 1909. Her unfortunate left turn could have been four or five miles southeast of Stonehouse, or the nearby Spring Valley Pony Express station.

96. Alice probably entered the old mining town of Ely over Aultman Avenue, then as now the town's principal street. She gave no clue as to her hotel—there were six in 1915. The Northern, on Aultman in the center of the business district at $1-$3 European, was listed first.

97. Alice ground her way over Robinson's Summit, Jake's Summit, White Pine Summit, and Pancake Summit—the road through the basin and range geology took on the aspect of a snapped bedsheet. The best hotel in Eureka was the Brown, next door to the Opera House. Both buildings are still standing and serving their original purpose, the Brown now an overflow adjunct to the Best Western.

98. The sand of western Nevada was an incredible obstacle to the automotive traveler. Her route took her by ruins of several Pony Express and Overland Stage stations—ruins that are still there. It took her over rugged mountain passes. Since Alice didn't mention the famous Frenchman station, she must have left

the route of the future Lincoln Highway east of there—possibly at Fairview—turning south for Rawhide. Fairview is only a mile off her route, but Rawhide is almost thirty miles away. But that way she could avoid the notorious stretches of loose sand that lurked to the west. She would have turned to enter Fallon from due south.

99. Alice would have hit the route of the future Lincoln Highway in Fallon, to turn west. The towns she mentioned are still there, and in Wadsworth she would have crossed the Truckee River very near the place where the covered wagon emigrants crossed it sixty years earlier. Sparks bursts out of the gloom even brighter today, as the travelers race down I-80, within a few yards of the path of the Maxwell.

100. The Riverside Hotel on Virginia Street still stands high above the Truckee River today, several remodelings after Alice reached it in 1909. It no longer accepts overnight guests.

11

Reno to the Golden Gate

STILL OVER two hundred miles from our destination, San Francisco, we could hardly contain ourselves with excitement as we prepared to enter the Golden State. Only a few more miles of Nevada remained.

William J. Mannix of Sacramento and T. F. Holmes of San Francisco had come to Reno for the express purpose of leading us up over the Sierra Nevada mountains and, by way of the Placerville mining section, downgrade through Sacramento to the western goal of all those many miles of travel.

Mr. Sharman had faithfully seen us through an heroic stage of that journey and would return to his native city beside the Salt Lake, while we again pressed onward. As we waved him an appreciative farewell, the Reno populace sent us off with cheers and good wishes for the remainder of the trip.

Our Golden Fleece was almost within our grasp. We did not confide our feelings to each other. There was great unspoken tenseness in this final lap of the long trek. As each passenger settled herself for the ride which would actually take us into California, I thought I could almost *hear* the sense of satisfaction silently breathed forth.

Southward upgrade to Carson City we proceeded, and lunched in a

Japanese restaurant where we learned of another earthquake in San Francisco—not a serious one, however. Looking out on the golden dome of the capitol building as we ate, we thought of all the strenuous life it had beheld in the latter half of the nineteenth century: hard-working miners, trying their luck at acquiring fortunes in a hurry; gay times and people, as a result of finding riches too rapidly; wild living, riotous brawls, murders, and resultant hangings. The rich production of the Comstock Lode had furnished much of the wherewithal for this fast, extravagant form of existence, remnants of which might still be seen, especially in the nearby ghost town, Virginia City. Carson City returned to normal activity and gradually took on more dignity.[101]

The Sierra range confronted us with sudden steepness as we started the climb to its crest soon after leaving the capital. The road was heavy with sand. This was in truth no automobile highway. It was an old wagon trail over the mountains and the grades were stiff. Traffic was largely trucking wagons and powerful horses, mules, or even oxen—sometimes just men in the saddle. First a long pull; then rest and cool off at the turn—only to double back up the side of the mountain at a constantly higher altitude. Those waits at the turns brought from each of us, "Oo-o, what a wonderful view." We ran out of superlatives. Ever since we crossed the Missouri River we had become more and more impressed by the vastness of things we saw—distances, mountains, and now trees. What clarity in the atmosphere and how the peaks stood out against the azure sky!

The carburetor was feeling the altitude, but the engine kept on pulling. That sturdy motor had been little short of wonderful in the way it plugged along, day after day, in mud, sand or heat. We simply marvelled at it. Various assembled parts had given trouble (showing evidence of not having reached full perfection in manufacture) but the motor was remarkably adequate to meet the exacting demands of that gruelling endurance test.

To give the engine all the ventilation possible we raised the sides of the hood and turned them back under. It was a noisy, rattling arrangement but the motor was grateful for the extra circulation of air and rewarded us by pulling all the harder if the grade demanded.

We mounted to considerable height in a comparatively few miles and finally attained a summit. There was a crude sign stating the altitude and we hopefully thought the long pull was over—and stopped to enjoy the sensation. Then we learned—there's another one beyond! Oh well, what's a summit or two more or less now? Victory was in sight. We had passed the worst of our road problems, and the heat too. All around us were mountain peaks and each time we stopped the views became more extensive and more gorgeous. Trees were plentiful and greener than we had seen for a long time. It was incredible that so soon after leaving that arid, barren desert we could be refreshed in the cool shade of towering evergreens. That was balm to our bodies and spirits. Even the inarticulate Maxwell appeared to echo our sensations.[102]

Beautiful mountains repay us for lots of discomfort.

Mounting the Glenbrook Grade (so they told us) we were not surprised to arrive before the Glenbrook Hotel, a large resort hostelry on the east shore of that magnificent gem, Lake Tahoe. Proceeding southward, the beautiful expanse of shimmering water bathed in the light of the descending sun and the numerous coves edged with dark green forests were delightful pictures bringing restful satisfaction.

Still gently ascending, we came at last to Lakeside Park at the southernmost tip of the lake where we found a lovely cottage reserved for our exclusive use. Here we could feast our eyes on exquisite loveliness.[103] Though we had covered but 70 miles—and it had taken eight hours to do it—they had been difficult ones and we felt we had earned the rest we enjoyed in this heavenly spot. Even a puncture just before arriving, failed to dim the pleasure of that glorious entrance to California.

Official summit of the Sierra Nevada Range near Lake Tahoe.

Majestic sugar pines, Douglas firs and redwoods lined our road on both sides. What a land! What mountains! What blue skies and clear, sparkling water! Our hearts leapt within us. None of us had ever seen the like— and we loved it. We almost chirped as we exclaimed over the grandeur that surrounded us on all sides. We started talking over plans when the trip was completed.

Nettie opened the discussion by remarking, "Maggie and I would like to see more of California before we go home."

"Yes, I can understand that, I'd like to, too," I said. "But we've been so much longer coming, that I'm not so sure, now."

"I don't know either," said Hermine. "Let's think it over and then talk about it again." That quieted things for the time being.

We were very surprised to find we had eleven more miles of ascent before we attained the height of the pass near Meyers. At this point we were at last in California and on the downward slope to the Pacific Coast.

We "oh"-ed and "ah"-ed at the handsome vistas as we skimmed along more gaily. The road was still narrow and the surface was a powdery kind of sand, but less deep. Our hearts grew lighter and lighter. Our difficulties were almost over and we would soon reach our goal. Any minor happenings now could not daunt our spirits.

Population was still pretty sparse until we approached Placerville, locally known as Hangtown. It had been camp headquarters for expectant miners who flocked to this area following the discovery of gold by James Marshall in 1848, at nearby Coloma.[104] Crime and lawlessness flourished along with the acquisition of easy money, and the attempt to ensure justice sometimes saw men hanged, not only singly, but in pairs. Evidently you had to be mighty well-behaved to escape with your life, one way or another! There were a few old prospectors still around "chawin" tobacco and looking as if they could tell some tall tales of the hangings they had luckily escaped.

Poor James Marshall—he only started out to build a saw-mill for Captain John Sutter, but he ended up with a wild and woolly town! Too intent on our immediate mission, we did not leave our path to visit Coloma. After spending the night in Placerville, we got away safely without any hanging![105]

Winding down through the hills at slightly lower altitudes, we came to Folsom where Mrs. Mannix, their young son Bill, Jr. and Mrs. Mannix's sister, Miss Louise Heilbron joined our caravan to their home in Sacramento.

As we entered Stockton the following day we were joined by a good-sized parade of automobiles around the city, their occupants cheering the Maxwell.

On either side of this community we encountered one of the earliest attempts at permanent Better Road improvement.

Near Hayward a terrific wind, gale-like in ferocity, accosted us and we feared we might actually lose our apparel; a good tight grip kept our birthday suits from showing!

Even as far back as 1909, the advertising profession would not have looked with approval on our entrance to the Golden Gate in the hours of darkness, so we spent the eve of our arrival in Hayward after a perilous snack of hot tamales and cheese omelettes![106]

Practically every day for the past two months we had had our stint of travel to perform. What would it feel like to arise to a day when, with our mission accomplished, we would no longer make a day's drive on the transcontinental trek? All the pent-up desire to see Bone and little John began to fill my thoughts rapidly with longing to return home. I could hardly wait to get back! The final twenty miles to the ferry house at Oakland gave my ardor plenty of opportunity to kindle, increased by the delay as we waited for the oncoming ferry to convey us across the Bay to San Francisco.

At last it arrived and we got aboard; but we left the automobile almost immediately to watch the final attainment of this long-elusive goal from the front end of the boat. People looked over the Maxwell, asked questions, and offered congratulations at its accomplishment.[107] Then the ferry-boat bumped against the piling of the slip and rocked a little as she slid in the opposite direction, finally snuggling into her resting place at the dock. As we drove into the street it was evident our arrival had been expected by a considerable crowd gathered in automobiles whose horns gave off repeated honks of welcome as the drivers squeezed the rubber bulbs. They kept up quite a din.

Finally a cavalcade of escorting Maxwells, occupied by Mr. Linz, District Manager of the Maxwell Company for the West Coast, Mr. and Mrs. Arthur Hull, with beautiful bouquets for us, and Mr. Ed Kelley and Mr. Mason doing their utmost to welcome us in the grand manner, led us up to the city proper.

Along the streets were Chinese, many with pigtails and native garb, others in the dress of their adopted country—more than we had ever seen in one place. People waved and cheered as we drove up Market Street.

Drawing up at the St. James Hotel[108] we were led in triumphal pro-

Waiting at Oakland, California, for the ferry to San Francisco—attainment of our goal.

cession to our suite of rooms where the reception continued for some time. We were joined there by photographers and press men, among them Charlotte Moyes, auto editor of the *Oakland Tribune*, all bent on recording the historic event.

What a day!

But, for that matter, what a journey!—a prelude to the thousands of women drivers who would later make this same trip—in *much* shorter time from Hell Gate to the Golden Gate!

The four of us—triumphant and happy.

Notes

101. Alice would have headed south on Virginia, the route of the Lincoln Highway from 1913 to 1920. Carson City was a little over thirty miles away on a fine graded dirt road. San Francisco was virtually wiped out by an earthquake, and subsequent fire in 1906.

102. Alice turned west at the Nevada state capitol on King Street, to head southwest

133

on the Kings Canyon Road. She emerged from the mountains at Spooner Summit a dozen miles to the south. They passed by Glenbrook, something that can't be done today as the Glenbrook Inn is in a gated area.

103. Alice would have entered the state of California near the present-day town of Meyers. Nearby Lakeside Park was on the Nevada-California line.

104. The Gold Discovery State Historic Park, with a working full-size replica of Sutter's mill, is at Coloma.

105. There were several hotels in Placerville in 1909, but Alice leaves no clue as to which one she used.

106. Like Placerville, Hayward listed four hotels in 1915, but again, Alice left no clue.

107. Although the Bay Bridge opened in the mid-1930s, the Oakland-San Francisco ferry was still in operation in post-war years. It docked at the Ferry Building at the Embarcadero, still on the San Francisco waterfront and recently restored.

108. The St. James Hotel was located at Van Ness and Fulton Streets, replaced in the late 1920s by the Veteran's Memorial Building.

EPILOGUE

AS THE fiftieth anniversary of the start of our historic journey rolled around, an article in the *New York Times* of Sunday, June 7, 1959, under the byline Joseph C. Ingraham awakened renewed interest. Mr. Ingraham had done research on records and photographs in the Automotive History Collection of the Detroit Public Library and wrote an excellent story. This was followed by many magazine and newspaper items across the United States. Through a letter of appreciation my daughter wrote to Mr. Ingraham while I was enroute home from the east, James J. Bradley of the Detroit Library learned of my residence in California. He wrote to me requesting photos and clippings of the original trip.

Subsequently an invitation to attend the 43rd National Automobile Show, held for the first time in Detroit in October 1960, brought me two awards at the Automotive Old Timers' luncheon. One of these was the handsome plaque from the AAA presented by its President, Charles Wilson. I am sure you can read the inscription on that. The other was a lovely blue leather scroll within which was a charcoal portrait of me and a beautifully composed letter signed and presented by Charles L. Jacobson, Vice President of Chrysler Corporation and Chairman of the Automobile Show Committee, and Harry A. Williams, Managing Director of the Automobile Manufacturers Association. I was completely surprised and deeply moved to receive these tokens of recognition. Though they are inscribed in my name, they represent more truly the complete co-operation of my three companions and of many others who contributed in one way or another to the success of our venture, whether it be those who launched the initial idea, the men in the factory who built the victorious car, or those who assisted along the way.

Only one of my companions of the road is now living, Nettie Powell

135

Charles L. Jacobson, Vice-President of Chrysler Corporation, Car W. Kelsey, proposer of my trip, myself, and Harry A. Williams, Managing Director of the Automobile Manufacturers Association, at the National Automobile Show, Cobo Hall, Detroit, October 20, 1960.

Lewis, who has passed her 101st birthday.[109] It is not difficult to compute m approximate age if the details in this volume are carefully put together!! I ar still driving across our land annually, sometimes oftener, and more than 2 different people have made the journey with me. Always I am thrilled an amazed that modern road improvements have not only shortened consider ably the 3800 miles of rough going, but that the distance which then cor sumed 41 days, can now be easily and comfortably traversed in a week more or less, depending on speed and the length of one's driving day. And a evening approaches one can be sure of Beautyrest mattresses and other luxu ries for the night's rest. Quite a change from the old days!

Epilogue

For all four of us I wish to express grateful thanks to everyone who had any part in our wonderful trip, many of whom remained unknown to us personally, and to the legion of friends whom we yet recall with pleasure. To all rightfully belongs the honor I gladly share. With them must also be included many who have aided in the publication of this story of the event.

It is a gratifying sensation to receive the recognition so generously bestowed upon us which has made proud and happy the heart of the author

ALICE H. RAMSEY.

Covina, California
September, 1961.

The plaque

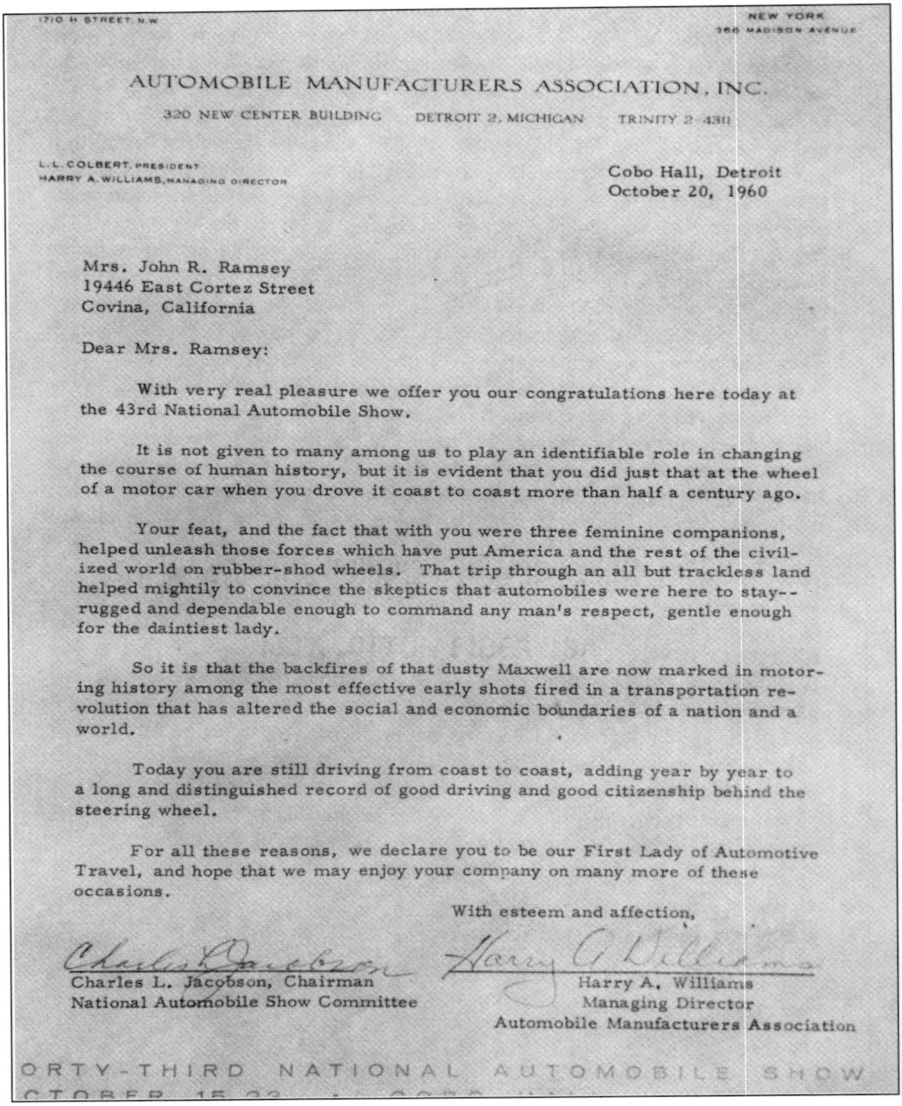

1710 H STREET N.W

NEW YORK
366 MADISON AVENUE

AUTOMOBILE MANUFACTURERS ASSOCIATION, INC.

320 NEW CENTER BUILDING DETROIT 2, MICHIGAN TRINITY 2-4311

L. L. COLBERT, PRESIDENT
HARRY A. WILLIAMS, MANAGING DIRECTOR

Cobo Hall, Detroit
October 20, 1960

Mrs. John R. Ramsey
19446 East Cortez Street
Covina, California

Dear Mrs. Ramsey:

With very real pleasure we offer you our congratulations here today at the 43rd National Automobile Show.

It is not given to many among us to play an identifiable role in changing the course of human history, but it is evident that you did just that at the wheel of a motor car when you drove it coast to coast more than half a century ago.

Your feat, and the fact that with you were three feminine companions, helped unleash those forces which have put America and the rest of the civilized world on rubber-shod wheels. That trip through an all but trackless land helped mightily to convince the skeptics that automobiles were here to stay--rugged and dependable enough to command any man's respect, gentle enough for the daintiest lady.

So it is that the backfires of that dusty Maxwell are now marked in motoring history among the most effective early shots fired in a transportation revolution that has altered the social and economic boundaries of a nation and a world.

Today you are still driving from coast to coast, adding year by year to a long and distinguished record of good driving and good citizenship behind the steering wheel.

For all these reasons, we declare you to be our First Lady of Automotive Travel, and hope that we may enjoy your company on many more of these occasions.

With esteem and affection,

Charles L. Jacobson, Chairman
National Automobile Show Committee

Harry A. Williams
Managing Director
Automobile Manufacturers Association

ORTY-THIRD NATIONAL AUTOMOBILE SHOW

The letter

Epilogue

Notes

109. Nettie lived to the age of 105.

Chasing Alice

  To both professional and amateur geographer-historians, there is a certain romance to pathways of the last two centuries. This hit in a big way in my studies of the Oregon and Santa Fe Trails of the 1840s-'60s, and it hit even bigger when it dawned on this writer that the Lincoln Highway, and roads of that era (1913-30) have become just as historic. And just as beckoning in the first years of this twenty-first century.

  I grew up in the little western Iowa town of Glidden, on US 30 today, but on the Lincoln Highway in earlier years. It must have been 1940 or '41 when my parents first let me hitchhike to Des Moines, and there was a curious sensation when, awaiting a ride, I would look down at the gravel on the shoulder of the road, wondering how many cars had passed that way in the days of the Lincoln Highway. Or how many buggies or Concord coaches had passed by in the pre-automobile age. Or how many Indians. Or how many buffalo.

  Much later I learned that the historic Lincoln Highway passed right up the main drag of Glidden in its first year, right past the grocery store being run by my grandfather, Ashton Marvin ("Toot") Henderson—a building which in recent times served as a hardware store owned by my brother, Rusty Franzwa. Toot fought hard to keep the Lincoln in town but the Detroit bigwigs would have none of that provincialism, so they routed it firmly and permanently on the north edge of Glidden.

  With the copyright for Alice Ramsey's Veil, Duster, and Tire Iron *long expired, it was decided that our Patrice Press should reprint the book, and we have done so verbatim. Except that we felt that it should be annotated, to give today's readers a more thorough insight into her adventures, and rather than clutter up the pages with footnotes, we elected to place them at the end of each chapter. None are attributive—all amplify Alice's text.*

But more is needed, and hence this appendix. "Chasing Alice," has been included, not just to document our own research, but to commend the several dozen enthusiastic contributors who have added so much to the book. Many are members of the new Lincoln Highway Association, working hard to elevate popular awareness of the pathway taken by Alice Ramsey nearly a century ago.

New Jersey

Alice was born to John and Ada Huyler on Nov. 11, 1886. John Rathbone Ramsey, the son of John and Martha Rathbone Ramsey, was born in Bergen County on April 25, 1862. He married his first wife, Mary, in 1893, and she died in 1898. A widower for eight years, he married Alice on Jan. 10, 1906. She was 20; he was 43. An attorney, he was the Bergen County Clerk from 1895 to 1910, and was president of the Hackensack Brick Co. from 1909. A director of several banks, he was elected as a Republican to the Sixty-fifth and Sixty-sixth U.S. Congresses, 1917-21. Their home, still standing, was on the corner of State and Lewis Streets in Hackensack, New Jersey. John Rathbone Ramsey died April 10, 1933, at age 70.

New York City

The photo on page 2 of Alice Ramsey's book clearly shows New York City's Maxwell dealership at 1930 Broadway, with the 1909 Maxwell DA pointed left, as Alice and her companions were ready to drive north to the state's capital city. That meant that the dealership was on the east side of Broadway. Attorney Sarah Johnson, who lives nearby on West End Avenue (between the Hudson River and Central Park), was asked to check it out. The daughter of Charles and Candace Franzwa Johnson of Tucson, Sarah frequently walks past that address and remembered that a high-rise apartment building occupied the site for many years. Construction has just been completed on a replacement apartment-retail tower on the northeast corner of Broadway and 64th Street, numbered (and named) 1930 Broadway.

Avery Fisher Hall, a component of Lincoln Center, is across Broadway from the site of Alice Ramsey's departure, now the heart of Manhattan's Upper West Side.

Readers who would like to follow Alice's precise path to Albany would have an interesting time of it. The ancient Albany Post Road and US 9, come close, but those roads aren't necessarily the same roads taken by our travelers. Those in a hurry could reach Albany in just a couple or three hours by driving the modern highways, and the traveler should be no more than a mile or two from the 1909 route for most of the way.

Almost all the roads taken by Alice still exist, and it should be possible to follow her route with precision for most of the way. There are a few places where modern

1930 Broadway in 2005

construction of limited access expressways have wiped out some of the route, but our text gives details for following the accessible portions of her route for today's adventurers.

Folks absolutely insisting on following Alice's exact route may want to copy the following 7.5-minute quadrangles of the USGS, which can be examined without charge either at a federal repository (such as a major US university or library) or on line.

Here is a list of those quadrangles, south to north: Central Park, Yonkers, White Plains, Ossining, Haverstraw, Peekskill, West Point, Wappingers Falls, Poughkeepsie, Hyde Park, Kingston East, Clermont, Hudson South, Stottville, Hudson North, Kinderhook, Ravena, East Greenbush, and Troy South.

Jim Powell found a map of the city dated 2005, which shows a couple of streets west of Broadway (US 9), between West 251st and 253rd, both labeled "Old Albany Post Road." Would these have been used by Alice in 1909? Probably not, but here is the map and a picture of a remnant between W. 251st and Lakeview Place.

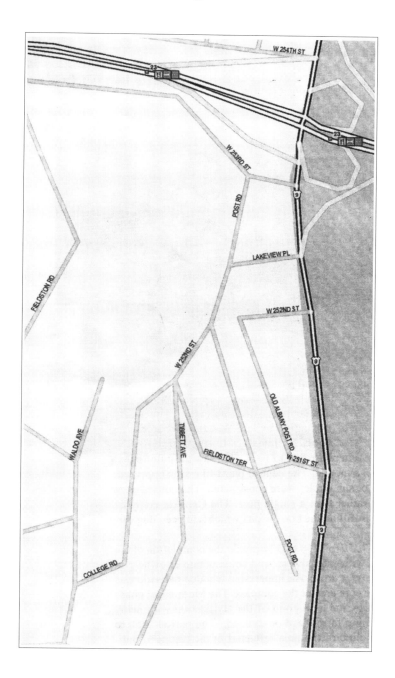

This remnant is between W. 251st Street and Lakeview Place.

Manhattan to Poughkeepsie

Getting Alice off Manhattan Island is no problem. She simply drove north on Broadway from the Maxwell dealership for some six or seven miles, crossing the Harlem River into the Bronx over the Broadway Bridge. That area is still known as Spuyten Duyvil, "spitting devil," the name given to a nearby creek by the pioneer Dutch more than four centuries ago.

Powell found *The Standard Road Book of New York State,* dated 1910, which supplies directions to follow present Broadway to Yonkers. That book simply advises travelers to stay on Broadway, right through the town, and Broadway, now also US 9, still goes through the heart of Yonkers.

However, he later found detailed driving directions from Manhattan to Albany published in 1910. These probably were very similar to the directions given to Alice in June 1909. From this it was learned that she probably left Broadway only a few blocks north of the bridge. She probably turned west on 230th Street in the Bronx, and that road ends just a few blocks ahead at Riverdale Avenue. Then she turned north on Riverdale to follow that street, rather than Broadway, into Yonkers.

Knowing of my frustration in the search for primary materials to establish Alice's route in 1909, Jim Powell found an incredible book, *The New York and Albany Post Road: From Kings Bridge [Broadway Bridge] to "The Ferry at Crawlier, Over Against Albany" Being an Account of a Jaunt on Foot Made at Sundry Convenient Times Between May and November, Nineteen Hundred and Five.* It was written by C. G. Hine, who lays on the history in more than one hundred pages of wonderful material. Here is an interesting passage:

> The [Albany] Post Road, known in these days as Broadway, follows the eastern edge of the Mosholu swamp to Van Cortlandt Park, through what is called the Vale of Yonkers. Here is Vault Hill, one of the points selected by Washington on which to make a display for the benefit of the British, while he quietly led his main army south for the operations against Cornwallis.

Bright as she was, Alice probably was unaware of the momentous happenings of more than 130 years earlier, as she plowed north through the rainy morning of April 9. Hines was walking along that road just four years earlier:

> ...as one approaches Dobbs Ferry he steps on almost holy ground. Here is the Livingston house, where, after the fighting was all over, Washington and Governor Clinton met the British commander, General Sir Guy Carlton, to make the final arrangements for peace...in which the British gave up all claim upon the allegiance and control of the country.

The Palisades, on the Jersey Shore of the Hudson, are at their best in this area. They are visible for a space of some fifteen miles, from 200 to 500 feet of basaltic rock with a columnar formation. This traprock once was molten lava, sunk into Triassic sandstone.

The Riverdale designation ends at Main Street in Yonkers, but Alice would have continued straight ahead on Warburton. Passing close to the Hudson River, she would have continued north on Warburton until it ends at Broadway, US 9. Then she would have turned left to continue north on US 9.

Alice's Drive

While they were in Tarrytown, one can't help but wonder if Alice or her companions were aware, as they were sipping their hot chocolate, that they were in the Philipse domain, home to both the capture of Major André and *The Legend of Sleepy Hollow.*

By the middle of the nineteenth century, Washington Irving was one of the most celebrated writers in the world. Students of the Oregon Trail should be familiar with his non-fiction works, *Astoria* and *The Adventures of Captain Bonneville,* as well as his still-popular short story, *The Legend of Sleepy Hollow.* By 1909 there probably wasn't a person in America who wasn't familiar with the gangly Ichabod Crane, Katerina Van Tassel ("plump as a partridge"), and the Headless Horseman.

After the women had finished their hot chocolate and resumed their rainy drive through Tarrytown, they passed Patriot's Park, where Major André was captured, and later hanged as a traitor. And also where Ichabod first caught sight of the Headless Horseman.

Then the Maxwell passed North Tarrytown (still today's US 9), since named Sleepy Hollow, and just north of town, the Sleepy Hollow Cemetery. Had Alice turned in there she could have crossed a bridge very near the one where HH bonked Ichabod with his punkin head. (Of course it was fiction, but the bridge wasn't, and the foundations of the old one are still visible from the deck of the new one.)

Irving spent the last years of his life in Tarrytown and in fact is buried in the churchyard of the old Dutch church, known today as Sleepy Hollow Cemetery. He died Nov. 28, 1859, aged 76.

Proceed north on US 9 to Ossining, overlooking the Hudson River's Tappan Zee, a widening of the Hudson River. Sing-Sing, the famous prison, was on the river bank here—in fact, until eight years prior to Alice's trip, Sing-Sing was the name of the town. When C. G. Hine walked through in 1905 he cited the town "as a resort for guests of the state."

Continuing north on US 9, the name of the road changes from Broadway to Albany Post Road when approaching the intersection of US 9 with NY 117. Nearing Crotonville NY 9A will come beneath US 9. The two will split about a mile to the northwest—slant to the left on 9A.

Alice followed what is now 9A through Croton-on-Hudson through Buchanan, and turned right on Welcher Avenue. The road goes beneath US 9. Then she would have turned left on Washington Street. She would have

146

followed Washington north into Peekskill, then slanted right on South Street, then left on Division Street.

They would have driven north on Division to the Civil War monument at Highland. And right here today's travelers need to make a decision. To the northeast a long dirt section of the oldest version of the Albany Post Road has been preserved, and although it is probable that Alice would not have gone on that ancient stretch, Powell feels that today's drivers might want to do so. The dirt stretch, never paved, is about 6.6 miles long and is listed on the National Register of Historic Places. Here are the directions he passed along to our readers:

Zero the odometer at the junction of Division and Highland. Don't touch it again for another 10.2 miles. Turn right on Highland. Here we go:

0.5 – Cross beneath Bear Mountain Parkway.

0.9 – Enter Courtlandt, where the name changes from Highland to Oregon Road.

1.5 – Pass Pierre Van Courtlandt House on left.

1.6 – Turn left on Gallows Hill Road

3.0 – Stop sign. Here the road name changes from Gallows Hill to Sprout Brook.

3.6 – Continental Village Monument and continue straight up the hill. The paved Sprout Brook Road (CR 13) bends to the right.

3.6 – Now on Old Albany Post Road. Continue on hard-packed dirt for 6.6 miles; note that the old stone mileposts are intact, starting with 53 (ca. 1760s—53 miles north of New York City.)

9.2 – Stop sign at Indian Brook Road. The 1756 Bird and Bottle Inn is on the left.

10.2 – The historic section ends and US 9 is joined—continue north on 9 to Fishkill.

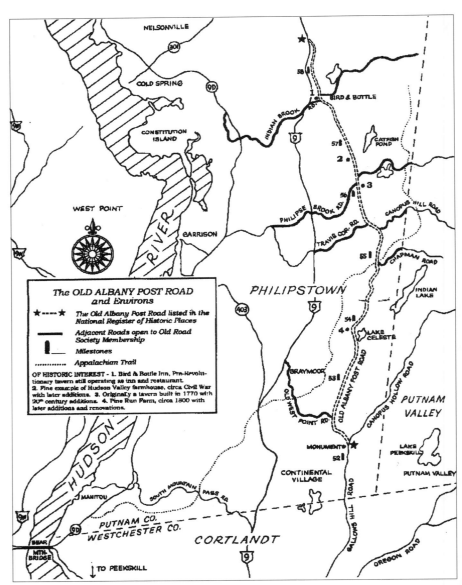

Jim Powell came up with this map, showing the "Old Albany Post Road" south of the Bird and Bottle Inn. The dirt section is shown as double dashed lines.

The eight-acre Bird and Bottle property, operating as a bed-and-breakfast inn, was sold at auction in May 2004 after the death of its owner. It was built in 1756 as Warren's Tavern, serving travelers on the Albany Post Road. It became a formal stop on the New York City to Albany stage road, when legislation establishing that road was established in 1785.

The Bird and Bottle was closed as of this publication and in the winter of 2004-05 was in the process of restoration.

Those who opt to skip the historic dirt road and follow Alice's path would want to follow Highland Avenue through Annsville, cross US 9, and turn right on the Albany Post Road. Rejoin US 9 and continue north to the junction with NY 403. Bear left there to the junction with NY 9D, Garrison Four Corners. Turn right on 9D toward Cold Spring. Entering Cold Spring, fork right on Peekskill Road to NY 301, Main Street. Turn right on NY 301 to the junction with US 9.

Turn left on US 9 and drive into Fishkill.

With the smooth tires and obviously no power steering, Alice's drive was a continuing fight, with a constant and tight grip on the steering wheel. So she could be forgiven if she failed to notice the towns she was passing as she proceeded north. That doesn't mean they weren't important. But keep in mind that it was raining, and the black pantasote top was only an inch or two above the heads of the passengers. An isinglass in windshield had been lowered to keep the rain out of Alice's face, and that would have further hampered visibility.

So she could be forgiven for not noticing some important historical villages, such as Peekskill, named for Jan Peek, a seventeenth century mariner who was such a souse that he ran his ship up the "kill," or brook, named for him, thinking it was the Hudson until he ran aground. The village was sacked and burned by the British in 1777, and the neighboring settlements pillaged.

Another town she didn't mention is Fishkill, the scene of incidents from James Fenimore Cooper's *The Spy.* Settled in 1682, it was the largest town in the county during the Revolution.

In Fishkill she would have left US 9 by turning right on Main Street. (Today, turn right on Elm and left on Main), then back across US 9 to Church Street. Rejoining US 9 she would have proceeded north across a high plateau for about six miles, to Wappingers Falls. There Alice probably slanted to the left on Old Route 9, then returned to US 9, which is East Main Street. She would have slanted off US 9 onto East Main, and followed that road to West Main Street, which is NY 9D. Then 9D would have been followed until it rejoined US 9, South Road, which would have been followed toward Poughkeepsie.

Nearing Poughkeepsie, when US 9 goes left, Alice's road would have continued straight ahead—South Avenue. She would have followed South directly to Market Street. She would have turned left on Main Street to arrive at Hotel Warner, where they stopped for the night.

The hotel boasted a café, grill, pool room and barbershop. It was next door to the Poughkeepsie Opera House.

The town was cited as a "safe harbor" by the Indians, where canoes were "safe from wind and wave," according to Hine. Rocky bluffs project into the river. The southern one was known to the Dutch as Call Rock. "From this rock old Baltus Van Kleek and his neighbors were wont to hail passing sloops for news or passage," Hine wrote.

Poughkeepsie to Albany

Collection of Gregory M. Franzwa

Poughkeepsie's Market Street would have looked like this a few years before Alice's arrival.

Collection of Gregory M. Franzwa

This is Poughkeepsie's Main Street, looking east. Market Street is a block ahead and the Nelson House is a half-block to the right. Alice turned right (to the left in this photo) at this corner to proceed north, toward Albany.

151

The great Nelson House was on Market Street, about a half-block south of Main. And the freshly cleaned automobile wouldn't be clean long. With the plastic windshield fluttering before them, Alice drove the clanking Maxwell north to the corner, the rain falling softly on the Pantasote top, turned left for a block and then right onto Washington Street, which today is NY 396.

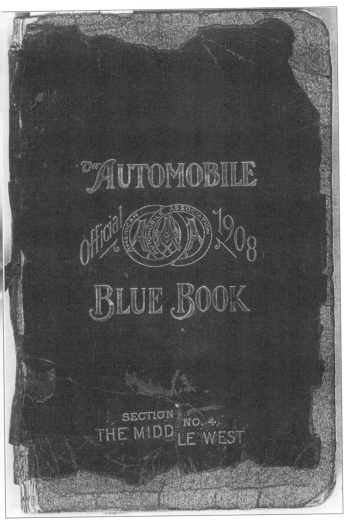

Nettie's Blue Book *was the 1908 New York volume, which would have had a cover similar to this one.*

Collection of
Michael E. Weigler

Soon the road joined present US 9 and the Maxwell continued north. A few miles ahead, approaching Staatsburg, present US 9 veers to the right, but Alice's route continued on Old Post Road through town, then rejoined US 9 northeast of the village, still headed north.

The Maxwell continued into Rhinebeck, and here is what our 1905 hiker, C. G. Hine, had to say about it:

Ryn Beck, Rein Beck, Rhynbeek, Reinebaik, Rhinebeck, was the name at first applied to that region back from the river and located on the property of William Beekman, which was occupied by the "High Dutchers," while in Kipsbergen, on the river bank, lived the "Low Dutchers."...

The view down the river from here is something never to be forgotten; the dazzling effect of the sun on the water, the hills of the further shore, and the grand expanse of the picture which is only limited by the condition of the atmosphere, must be seen to be appreciated.

Hine found gravestones in the Lutheran Church burial ground north of town dating to 1733.

In Rhinebeck, fronting US 9 is the Beekman Arms Inn. Dating from 1766, it is the oldest hotel in continuous operation in the United States. When Alice passed by, it was known as the Rhinebeck Hotel, but it was already billed in the *Blue Book* as "The Oldest Hotel in America."

North of Rhinebeck, where US 9 bends to the right, Alice followed Montgomery Street into the Old Post Road, then continued northeast to rejoin present US 9, to the north. She stayed on US 9 north through Red Hook to the junction with CR 31, the site of Blue Stores. That is on the left side of US 9, a little more than three miles into Columbia County. Alice would have turned left there on CR 31 to follow the road over to US 9. Then she would have turned right to enter Hudson on Worth Avenue, but still US 9. Now US 9 wiggles around in Hudson, and where it turns left, Alice probably turned right on Prospect Avenue, right on Columbia Street and right on Fairhaven Avenue, which becomes US 9. Follow it north to Kinderhook.

C. G. Hine found the Kinderhook area charming: "[Approaching Kinderhook] there is plenty of time to view the beauties of nature and fill one's nostrils with its rich perfumes. Most of the year's work in the fields is finished…"

The retirement home of ex-president Martin Van Buren is on the

Alice's Drive

Albany Post Road, US 9, some two miles north of Kinderhook. Washington Irving stayed there often, and C. G. Hine writes that it was here that he became acquainted with the schoolteacher Jesse Merwin, prototype of Ichabod Crane. From Hine:

> A step further on, and across the highway, stands the Katrina Van Tassel house, on whose blooming young mistress the Yankee pedagogue was wont to cast longing eyes.

Entering town on Broad Street (US 9), Alice probably turned left on Hudson Street, also CR 21. At a fork, where CR 21 bends left, she would have followed the Old Post Road to the right to NY 9H, then turned left on 9H, almost immediately rejoining US 9 north. She then would have continued northeast to the point where US 9 joins US 20, the Columbia Turnpike. Today you turn left at the junction and follow the Columbia Turnpike through Schodack Center and East Greenbush, then cross the Hudson River on US 9 and 20, the new Dunn Bridge. Alice would have crossed on the now-gone East Greenbush Bridge, whose abutments are just downstream.

For the record, here is the now-impossible 1909 route: Just two blocks south of present Rensselaer, the Albany Post Road, US 9 today, ended—right on the banks of the Hudson River. Alice would have turned right there on Broadway and driven into Rensselaer. She would have turned west there at the trolley tracks and mounted the East Greenbush Bridge. At the east end of the bridge she would have jogged to the left, still following the trolley tracks, and entered Ferry Street.

The very capable historian of the city of Albany, Virginia B. Bowers, was most helpful in charting Alice's route to the west.

Alice and her companions would have driven west along Ferry Street for a few blocks to Pearl. Then right on Pearl to State, left on State to Eagle, right on Eagle, and immediately she angled left onto Washington.

These directions are given because the Albany city directories for 1908 and 1910 do not disclose the location of a Central Garage, where the travelers met their escort and advance man, J. D. Murphy.

Ultimately they all would have reached Washington Avenue, and from there they would have headed west. Washington becomes Central and later NY 5, which was followed all the way to Schnectady.

154

Taken from Albany looking east, this is the Old Greenbush Bridge. Alice would have come across and jogged left (right in this view) for a short distance before proceeding west on Ferry Street.

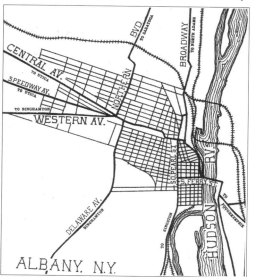

This map of Albany is from The Standard Road-Book of 1910.

One could deduce that, despite the fact that she was driving roads unfamiliar to her, Alice made good time from Poughkeepsie to Albany. She was still fighting the wheel and the weather but she probably got there around noon on Thursday, June 10. Rather than waste several hours of daylight, she elected to continue west in the rain.

Albany to Auburn
It is possible that Alice could have gained the north bank of the Mohawk River by driving north from Albany, but Virginia Bowers is of the opinion that she would have driven the more popular road west, identified today as NY 5, to Schenectady, to cross just west of that city.

The fifteen-mile drive would have taken the travelers into Schenectady over present Albany Street, passing through the central business district and beneath the railroad overpass to the end of the street. There the Maxwell would have been turned to the right to cross the toll bridge across the Mohawk. It's a good bet that JD had already paid the toll and proceeded ahead by train.

Across the river Alice turned left to follow the road, still NY 5, to the west. The adventurers entered Amsterdam some fifteen miles to the west, on Main Street. Present maps of the town show Main Street disappearing, with a split in the east part of town. A good guess would have Alice bearing to the left, along the riverfront, but this is now a one-way street eastbound. The northern loop, one-way westbound, joins the southern one on West Main Street.

Amsterdam got its present name in 1808, but prior to that time there were only a few primitive buildings on the site. The first bridge across the Mohawk was built in 1821. The town has been noted as a carpet manufacturing center, but now the mills are all closed. It's a city of about 20,000 people today.

According to the 1910 *Standard Road-Book*, Alice would have followed Main Street to Market, jogged to the right a block and turned left onto Division. She evidently followed that for just one block to Clinton, then turned left onto Guy Park.

It was still cloudy when the women left Hotel Warner on Saturday morning, June 12, and Alice still had to fight the steering wheel after several

Collection of Gregory M. Franzwa

This view of East Main Street, Amsterdam, looks west. The postcard was produced before the turn of the twentieth century, but the street would have been little changed in 1909.

days of soaking rain. It would have been a joyful moment for the passengers when the clanking chains were removed and the constant shaking and rumbling gave way to a relatively smooth ride on the hard-packed dirt.

This advertisement was published in the 1908 Blue Book.

VARIABLE WEATHER
or
STEADY BAD WEATHER

do not produce road conditions so muddy, snowy, or slippery that

WEED CHAIN TIRE GRIPS

will not render automobiling *possible* and *enjoyable*, and *safe* from dangers of skidding and slipping. Suit-able for *all seasons.*

FOR SALE BY DEALERS EVERYWHERE

MANUFACTURED BY

Weed Chain Tire Grip Co.

28 Moore Street   New York, N. Y.

157

The 1910 *Standard Road Book* states that the Mohawk River would have been followed to the west, with a left turn taking travelers to Fonda, forty-two miles from Albany. The road forked to the left just beyond the railroad station, leading through Yosts, Sprakers, Palatine Bridge, Nelliston, and St. Johnsville, to Little Falls, seventy-two miles from Albany. Alice would have driven through Little Falls along the railroad tracks to Albany Street in Herkimer. At the Herkimer railroad station, she probably turned right onto Church Street to go through Schuyler to Deerfield, and at the "Four Corners" turned left to cross the flats to Utica, on Genesee Street, ninety-six miles west of Albany.

Martin House was on Bleecker Street in Utica, a site now occupied by the Utica School of Commerce. This 1916 photo shows a newer Martin House on the left, but Alice and her companions dined in the old structure, on the right. Martin House was razed in 1966.

Continuing west on NY 5, the Maxwell would have plunged into the heart of Syracuse, turning south for a block and one-half to the Hub, on East Washington Street. They would have continued on NY 5 as it looped to the southwest to enter Auburn.

Auburn's Osborne House still stands, or at least the lower half of it does. Ormie King, Auburn's leading historian, says that the remainder of the structure now serves as a home for less affluent citizens. Alice would have continued through the center of the business district to the hotel, on the corner of State and Green Streets. Today's drivers will find that Route 5 is now also US 20, the major highway having joined the state route just east of the city.

Collection of Ormie King

The Osborne House was Auburn's leading hotel in 1909.

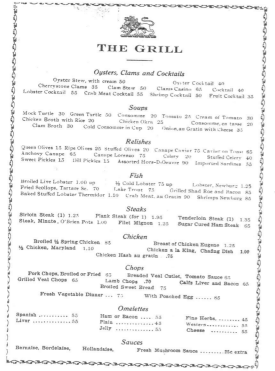

The Grill menu at the Osborne House featured a variety of dishes, including lobster for a dollar and up, and jelly omelettes for fifty-five cents.

Collection of Ormie King

Auburn to Chicago

Copper John has stood sentry over the Auburn Correctional Facility since 1821, when he was mounted atop the prison's first administration building. In 1848 he was replaced by a replica made of sheet copper. Removed in the late 1930s when the original building was being rebuilt, there was some consideration of displaying the statue at the New York World's Fair until examination disclosed that it was "anatomically correct." In a restoration which took place early in 2005, prison officials decided to render the statue anatomically *in*correct, prompting manufacture of T-shirts protesting the alteration: "Save Copper John's Johnson." Remounting the statue atop the building is scheduled for September 2005.

Until the advent of electronic ignition in recent years, automobiles needed coils to amplify the electrical charge to the distributor, and then to the spark plugs. No coil, no spark, and a dead engine.

Following Route 5, Alice would have entered Buffalo from the northeast, curving down to the central business district where Route 5 and Main Street are the same.

The 1908 Blue Book carried this map of Buffalo. Alice would have entered the city on the looping road labeled as Main Street.

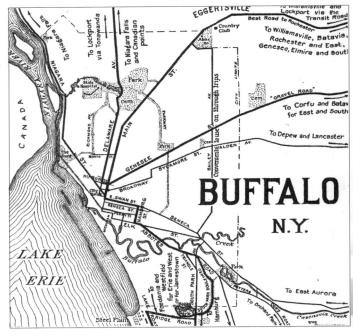

Collection of Gregory M. Franzwa

This postcard shows Buffalo's Iroquois Hotel ca. 1910.

Collection of Gregory M. Franzwa

The east side of Buffalo's Main Street looked like this about 1909,
with the Iroquois Hotel dominating the scene.

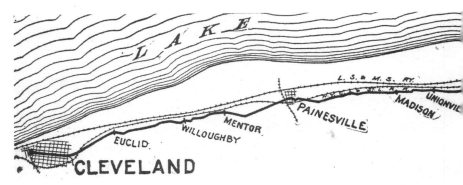

This map appeared in the 1908 Blue Book, *and depicts*

The 1908 Blue Book *carried this map of Cleveland. The Hollenden House was in the center of the business district.*

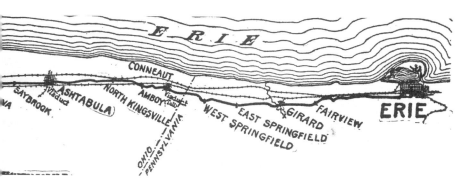

the road Alice probably traveled from Erie, Pa., to Cleveland.

The Hollenden House inserted this full-page ad in the 1908 Blue Book.

The Hotel Hollenden was opened in 1885 as Cleveland's most luxurious hotel. It was expanded to 1,000 rooms by a 1926 addition.
Western Reserve Historical Society

There was a sudden fad for after-market musical horns for a few years after World War II. The most common makes had a four-button "keyboard" which could be mounted on the steering column, and on which sports could play "Merrily We Roll Along" ad nauseum. The Cleveland Parkway was between Cleveland and Toledo.

It is obvious that the DA was equipped with a speedometer/odometer, an after-market addition. The advertisement on the facing page appeared in the 1908 *Blue Book*.

A 1909 Maxwell DA is now being restored by Rich Anderson, of Monroe, Wash. Quoting Rich:

The original illustrated parts manual I have for the 1909 DA does not show a speedometer. I believe common practice back then was to add items like that aftermarket. I'm certain Maxwell didn't supply one, but I'm sure Alice added one after she got the car, since the odometer on the speedometer would also be useful to her. In her book she talks about making some changes to the car, like adding a bigger gas tank, two spare tires, a running board toolbox, and the luggage rack on the back. So I would expect that she had a speedometer/ odometer also. Our car has one, and a clock also.

Collection of Gregory M. Franzwa

This real-photo postcard of Toledo's Boody House was produced in 1910, a year after Alice and her friends arrived there.

Alice's route would have joined the path of the future Lincoln Highway about here, just southeast of Ligonier, Ind. This 2002 photo shows the brick surface, laid in the early 1920s. The road was graded dirt when Alice arrived in 1909.

Gregory M. Franzwa

166

The first guidebook published by the Lincoln Highway Association was issued in 1915. Here is the ad inserted for the hotel in Goshen, Indiana, patronized by Alice and her companions on the night of June 17, 1909:

The Alderman

Formerly Hotel
HASCALL

American plan
Running water in every room

On the Lincoln Highway
North side Court House, Public Square   GOSHEN, IND.

The 1908 *Blue Book* offers a small-scale map of a route from South Bend to Chicago:

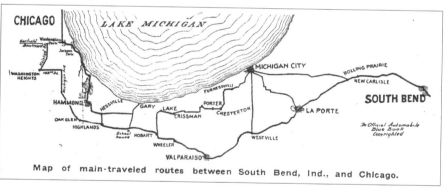

Map of main-traveled routes between South Bend, Ind., and Chicago.

Louis Chevrolet powers his Buick along the Crown Point racecourse.

The 1908 *Blue Book* carried a full-page detailed map of Chicago, both entering and leaving:

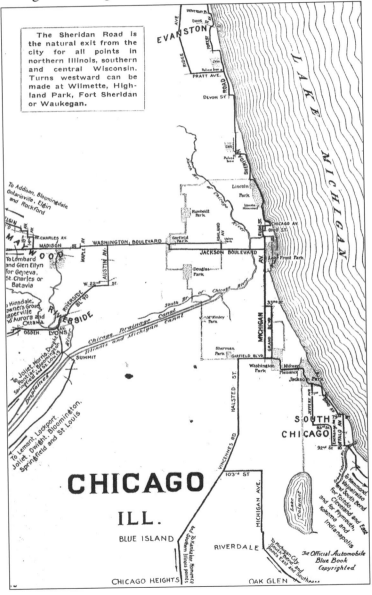

The "tunic coat" Alice donned as she left Chicago was probably a duster, a common item of apparel worn by all motorists when traveling the dusty roads in the open cars of the day. This ad appeared in the 1908 edition of the *Blue Book:*

Chicago to the Mississippi River

The people advising Alice on the road through Illinois were sending her along the route that would become the Lincoln Highway in 1913. Two years later, in 1915, the Lincoln Highway Association published the first of five guides entitled *The Complete Official Road Guide of the Lincoln Highway,* reprinted in 2002 by Tom Lutzi and still in print. (No longer at the original cover price of 50¢, but still a bargain at $16.95 postpaid. The book is available from the Lincoln Highway Trading Post, http://www.LHTP.com, or 1/800/454-8319.)

None of the five editions (1915, 18, 20, 21, and 24) tell where to turn to follow the precise route of the highway, but all give considerable information of interest to the traveler. The entry for Geneva, Ill., for instance, advises that the town is 941 miles west of New York City and 2,443 east of San Francisco. The name and rate of the only hotel appears, and the price of gas (16¢) is listed, along with washing and storage. The speed limit was 10 mph and it was enforced (meaning the town could afford a cop). There were 100 automobiles in the town of 2,800 people in 1915, and the route west was described as "Generally excellent gravel roads."

All tires in the era contained rubber tubes, and getting to them to repair a leak ranged from difficult to nearly impossible. The rubber patch Alice applied was coated with contact cement, and the pressure of the air in the tube generally would keep it adhered over the hole. In 1919 Robert M. Bowes began marketing a kit, with a rough-up cap. Included was a metal tin filled with a flammable paste. When placed over the treated rubber patch and lighted, the heat from the burning chemical would vulcanize the patch to the tube. Continuing under the banner, "Bowes Seal Fast," the firm is still prospering.

"Good Medicine for a Sick Horse" was a promotional painting for Bowes Seal Fast.

Automobiles prior to the 1980s were not gifted with fuel injection. Carburetors frequently required adjustment, particularly when changing altitude, such as crossing mountain ranges.

The little town of Malta, Ill., pop. 450 in 1915, probably would not have been noticed by Alice, but it was of great importance to the Lincoln Highway proponents, for this was the site of the historic highway's first "seedling mile." The LHA officials had arrangements with cement manufacturing firms to donate several carloads of cement to a community, if the local people would provide the sand, gravel, and labor to pave one mile of concrete. The location had to be out of town, and preferably in a low area that was prone to muddiness. The seedling mile in Malta opened in 1914. Drivers would plow through the mud and mount the slab, only ten feet wide. They would open the windshield and step on the gas, riding on the concrete carpet for a high-speed mile, then plunk right back down in the mud again. It was a convincing argument.

Collection of Gregory M. Franzwa

Malta's main street looked like this when Alice drove through.

Special Collections, University of Michigan Library

Six years after the Maxwell ground past this spot, the road looked like this. The 1915 photograph was taken fifteen miles east of Rochelle, Ill.

Former mayor Bob Gingerich knows that there were two hotels in Rochelle when Alice passed through on Tuesday, June 22. Alice didn't provide a name, but her scrapbook provided a picture. The older building was frame, but the Maxwell is shown parked in front of a masonry structure, certainly the Collier.

This ad appeared in the 1924 edition of The Complete Official Road Guide to the Lincoln Highway.

Although her first book, *Emily Post's Etiquette*, wouldn't be published until 1922, Emily was very much a lady in 1915, when she tried to drive from New York to the Panama-Pacific Exposition in San Francisco. She got a foretaste of trouble in Rochelle, when her monstrous British car became wedded to the mud of central Illinois. After two days of steady rain, the sun came out, a set of chains went on, and Emily and her companions churned on toward the West.

Special Collections, University of Michigan Library

Alice's route some fifteen miles east of the Iowa state line looked something like this.

Fulton's population six years after Alice passed through was 2,174. There were two hotels and three garages, and gas was 15¢ a gallon. In 1915 the toll bridge charged 15¢ a car plus a nickel a passenger. When J.D. was close at hand, it can be presumed that he paid all the food, lodging, and transportation costs, but he wasn't always close at hand. Although her book gives no clue, she had to have a substantial amount of cash with her, and certainly would have been reimbursed for her out-of-pocket expenditures by the Maxwell organization from time to time during the trip.

Not once in her book did she mention stopping for fuel. There probably wasn't a single filling station along her route—gasoline in those days usually was dispensed at lumber yards or hardware stores.

The Lyons and Fulton Bridge was ten years old when the travelers crossed the Father of Waters. It looked fragile but it survived without mishap for eighty-four years. The Maxwell might have been purring but there would have been a lot of noise as it rumbled over the plank decking. Once across the Mississippi River, there was a sharp right turn to the tollhouse—then a long, gentle slope to terra firma. A left turn brought the Maxwell into Lyons, annexed several years later by Clinton.

Lincoln Highway. Lyons High Bridge, over Mississippi River to Clinton, Iowa.

Collection of Gregory M. Franzwa

The Lyons and Fulton Bridge, viewed from the Iowa side.

The east abutments to the Fulton-Lyons Bridge were about a block north of Fulton's gigantic windmill.

174

By 1924 there was a second Mississippi River bridge into Clinton, so the owners of the official Lincoln Highway bridge took out this full-page ad in the Road Guide.

The Mississippi River to Boone, Iowa

It is sixty-one miles from Clinton to Mechanicsville, according to the LHA's *Road Guide* for 1915. Mechanicsville had a population of 871 in that year, and the Page Hotel charged $2 a night, presumably per room. The speed limit was 10 mph but the *Road Guide* said that it was not enforced. The Maxwell's top was up, but the need to seek shelter quickly probably saw the car exceeding the speed limit.

The situation confronting the travelers screamed for more research. We could locate no contacts in Mechanicsville, but one of the staffers at the courthouse in nearby Mount Vernon happened to live there, so a request for help was dispatched. There was no response.

The need for the name of a Mechanicsville contact was forwarded to Van and Bev Becker, of nearby Cedar Rapids. (Van is a national officer with the LHA.) Their report is printed here verbatim:

We were hot on the trail of the 1909 traveler and adventurer, Alice Ramsey, author of *Veil, Duster, and Tire Iron*. Like a gauntlet, Greg [Franzwa] had thrown down the challenge regarding Alice's rainy entry into Mechanicsville, Iowa.

We crossed the Union Pacific Railroad tracks carefully. We looked both ways—twice. Locals say there are seventy-five Union Pacific trains a day through eastern Iowa. These tracks would have been Chicago and Northwestern rails in 1909 as Alice Ramsey traveled west, heading for San Francisco. The road into Mechanicsville from the east was soon to become the Lincoln Highway, but not yet. Even today the best description of this road is graded dirt. The gravel has disappeared into the Iowa gumbo. Then, as now, the main street through town is known as First Street.

We had three objectives; find the Page Hotel, the livery stable, and the City Restaurant. Can we find them? Are they still there? The gray winter sky was darkening early in the afternoon. Daylight was fading fast. Was the trail from 1909 still warm? Have the tracks from Alices's venerable Maxwell vanished after these ninety-five years?

The first and easiest to find landmark is the Page Apartments, previously the Page Hotel. About 1959 the historic brick building at 219 First Street was remodeled, converting nine hotel rooms into five apartments. The front ground floor windows were updated about this time. The hotel was originally owned by the Page family. The daughter of the original owners, Virginia (Pagie) Page, lived to be 101 years old and is the one responsible for the transformation of the hotel in the 1950s.

The photo below, ca. 1909, shows Pagie in a pony cart in front of the hotel where Alice and her three companions spent the night.

The livery stable location required more investigation. The thriving community has had three or four livery stables. But in 1909, the only one in business was three doors west of the hotel. If Alice Ramsey parked her Maxwell inside to avoid a thunderstorm, it had to be the stable at 211 First Street. This conveniently located livery stable building is now the home of Bubba's, a tavern. The building is still there—even the 100-year-old concrete ramp from the sidewalk level up to the first floor level of the old livery stable. Over the years, a brick front has been added, and neon beer signs glowed in the windows of the gathering December gloom.

The café known as the City Restaurant in 1909 was also close at hand. It occupied a building with the letters RIBCO molded into the high front façade. The original business there was the Rock Island Brewing Company, evolved from a brewery to a tavern. The noise from this drunken tavern was so loud that hotel guests complained that they could not sleep.

The Pages solved the problem. They bought the building and converted it to the City Restaurant. The vintage photo below shows the City Restaurant with locals Belle Butler and Gene Onstott out front. That building, at 215 First Street, is now occupied by a chiropractor.

City Restaurant
Belle Butler and Gene Onstott pictured here in 1911

Sandwiched between the Page Hotel and the City Restaurant was a small barbershop, which has since evolved into a beauty salon.

The owners of the Page Apartments today are the granddaughters of the original owners of the Page Hotel. They own the three buildings we were looking for—hotel, restaurant, and livery stable. In the 1950s a brick front was added to the strip of buildings just west of the Page, covering the RIBCO logo. Alice's visit to Mechanicsville was four years before the street through this thriving community was designated as the official route of the Lincoln Highway. Look at that photo of Pagie and the pony cart. The buildings shown on the next page are from left to right the three businesses Greg Franzwa asked us to research. They are the Page Hotel, then a barbershop, the City Restaurant, and the livery stable.

But wait, there's more! Greg Franzwa said that Alice's visit occurred the third week of June 1909. Close. Alice Ramsey and her three female companions signed into the Page Hotel on June 23, 1909. The four guests indicated their home addresses were all in Hackensack, N.J. Of the four women, Alice signed last, as Mrs. John Ramsey. They stayed in Rooms 5 and 6 on the second floor. Alice stayed in Room #6, in the corner room overlooking the soon-to-be Lincoln Highway. They left a wake-up call for 5

The Page Apartments, formerly the Page Hotel in 1909
Van and Bev Becker

In 1909, the City Restaurant occupied this building with the awning.
Van and Bev Becker

The livery stable where Alice and her companions took refuge from the storm now houses a tavern.

Van and Bev Becker

A.M. They obviously needed a full day to make the twenty-five-mile trip to the big city to the west, Cedar Rapids. We took a photo of the hotel register so Greg Franzwa could see for himself.

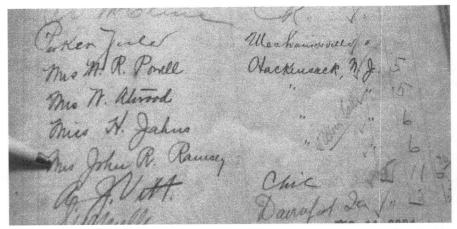

Van and Bev Becker

This hotel in the bustling community of Mechanicsville, Iowa, also hosted Bob Hope years later, as he waited for parts to repair his broken-down car. Sooner or later, the lure of the Lincoln Highway drew them all.

How did we find this information? Where did we begin? It all started with a telephone call. Bev remembered an assistant chief at the Cedar Rapids Police Department, where she works, who commutes from his home in Mechanicsville. A call to Bruce Kern yielded a single name and telephone number. Just one lead to follow.

Driving into town from the east, we easily located the Page Hotel, but where were the livery stable and City Restaurant? We hadn't a clue. A quick call to our one lead, Marie Cook, led to a friendly invitation to come visit at her home. Marie loved to talk about the old days in her beloved Mechanicsville. The visit provided insights and vintage photos and news articles from her extensive collection. One photo pointed us to the City Restaurant, but she was unable to answer some of our questions. Grabbing her telephone and pointing out a back window toward another house, she said, "Ginny would know."

Soon we were visiting in the home of Virginia and Bill Woods. Ginny

180

is a granddaughter of Alice and Bill Page, the original owners of the Page Hotel. She and husband Bill provided more information and photos than we had dreamed of. The real jackpot was the Page Hotel's old gold-embossed registers. With the help of Bill and Ginny, we located the entries in the old register of Alice Ramsey and her three traveling companions.

We reprinted the entire illustrated report here, to document the kind of help received all along the way. None as extensive in writing as the Beckers, but many who went the extra research miles for us.

The Beckers came through again in their hometown, Cedar Rapids. Alice stayed in the Hotel Montrose—the hotel's ad from the 1924 *Road Guide* is reproduced here:

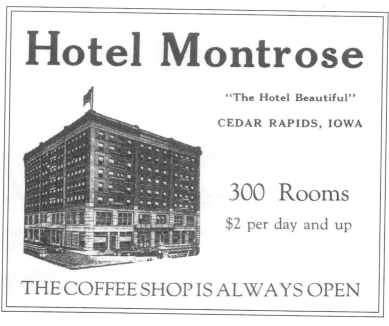

We asked for help on the hotel:

The Montrose Hotel in Cedar Rapids is definitely out of business. It was demolished to below ground level about fifteen years ago. Absolutely all remains are gone. In its place is a modern "City Center." That's fancy name for an upscale office building. The Montrose was on the corner of Third Avenue and Third Street SE. (All Cedar Rapids addresses are followed by the quadrant of the city.) The Lincoln Highway ran through downtown Cedar Rapids initially on First Avenue until the late 'teens, and then the maps show it coming through downtown on Second Avenue. The Montrose was one to two blocks off the mapped highway route. There are, however, photos and postcards of businesses on Third Avenue and nearby downtown streets that claimed to be "on the Lincoln Highway." I guess 100 years ago, close was good enough. In the mid-teens, the Montrose was one of the city's nicer hotels. You could spend the night for $1.50 up. For another $1.50 you could get your car washed at one of the local garages.

Collection of Van and Bev Becker

A real-photo postcard view of Cedar Rapids's Montrose Hotel, shown a few years prior to the arrival of Alice Ramsey.

Alice's description of Iowa's roads was no exaggeration. They were simply awful up until the early 1920s, when the state legislature passed laws enabling them to be rendered passable in wet weather.

The following photo, probably in the eastern part of the state, was taken a decade after the Maxwell churned through.

Collection of Gregory M. Franzwa

Youngville, mentioned in note 59, is something of a miracle in fundraising and historic restoration. The old combination home, café, and gas station was erected in 1931 by J. W. Young, but was a derelict by the early 1990s. Through diligent efforts by amateur fundraisers and volunteer

Youngville looked like this in 1994.
Gregory M. Franzwa

workmen, it has been restored to its former glory and is open at least two or three days a week. Proceeds from the sale of home made pie and coffee, plus a farmers market, take care of maintenance costs. It is on the northeast corner of US 30 and 218. It's a good idea to zero the odometer there and look for the bridge over Weasel Creek 1.5 miles to the west on US 30.

Gregory M. Franzwa

The restoration of Youngville was nearing completion when the photo above was taken in 2003.

Belle Plaine's Herring Hotel looked like this in 1994.

184

The Herring Hotel and Garage with Filling Station
BELLE PLAINE, IOWA
Half way House between Chicago and Omaha. Most congenial spot on the Highway. Opie Read styled it "A Bright Spot in the Desert".
Most cordially
Will P. Herring & Son
Jim Herring, Mgr.

Larry Adams, curator of the Mamie Doud Eisenhower Birthplace, Boone, gave us the information in note 63 on Boone's Northwestern Hotel.

Boone to Vail, Iowa

The agonizing decision made, Alice's companions would have had no trouble finding the ticket window, in the same building as their hotel; or the boarding platform, right out the back door.

Danger Hill has been tamed, but it is still very much a hill. The remains of a motel, long abandoned and now a derelict, are atop the rise.

Even well into the era of the Lincoln Highway a dozen or more years after Alice's drive, the road was a menace during each spring. Automobiles, trucks, and buses often had to be hauled out of the gumbo by teams of draft horses.

Alice left Jefferson at 4:30 on Sunday afternoon, June 27, heading for Carroll. We asked Bob Owens, who lives on the Lincoln Highway in Jefferson, to check the appropriate issue of the *Jefferson Bee,* June 30, 1909, and this is what he found:

WOMAN IN A LONG TRIP

3,700 miles in automobile
Passed through Jefferson last Sunday
on route from New Jersey to Los Angeles, California

Mrs. John R. Ramsey of Hackensack, NJ was in Jefferson Sunday afternoon on her way from the Atlantic coast to Los Angeles, California, in a 30 horsepower Maxwell touring car. If Mrs Ramsey succeeds in her attempt, which she says she certainly will do, she will be the first woman to drive a motor car across the continent. She is a little woman, not much over five feet in height, good-looking, refined, and one of the most enthusiastic motorists who ever visited Jefferson.

After considerable research by Norma Berns, it was learned that Alice stayed in Carroll's Burke Hotel, 6th and Main Streets.

They telephoned from Boone Saturday night to Mr. Haag (he had written to the party before they left New York and invited them to be his guests while in Jefferson) and told him they thought they would be here about noon Sunday. After dinner (noon meal) they had not appeared, so he took his car and went to the Boone county line to meet them. They arrived there at 4 p.m., having spent the day in the mud of Boone county, which Mrs. Ramsey said was the limit. After meeting Mr. Haag they drove to Jefferson over Greene county roads in [word unreadable] and after taking lunch, Mr. Haag piloted Mrs. Ramsey to Carroll, making the trip in an hour and forty minutes. She was loud in her praises of Greene county roads, which though pretty muddy and sticky in some places, she pronounced the first real roads she had seen since she left Cedar Rapids.

Anticipating a bad trip from Boone to Omaha, Mrs. Ramsey's three companions deserted her at Boone, and took the train for Omaha, where they were to meet her on arrival. She was accompanied through Jefferson by the man who looks after the car at night, keeping up with the party by train for this purpose. She expected to reach Omaha Monday night, and from there westward the roads are always dry and good at this season of the year. She was a fearless, rapid driver, and on the trip to Carroll Mr Haag said that with his new Maxwell roadster-30 he could run away from her on the fine smooth roads, but when the road was heavy she crowded him to keep out of her way.

Mrs. Ramsey started out to prove that the combination of a reliable car and a woman who knows it, can make the trip between the two oceans as well as any man. The trip, by the way, is wholly the result of this desire on the part of Mrs. Ramsey, coupled with her desire to see the country properly, from a motor car.

To date Mrs. Ramsey who, by the way, will make all the repairs on the car, had had little or nothing to do in this respect, the only trouble so far being two or three punctures and blowouts, which the little lady repaired herself on the road.She has driven the car every mile of the way herself. Her car weighs, when loaded with passengers and baggage, 3,500 pounds.

So far, and for some time to come, the party will put up at hotels on the way, but later on expect to do some camping, and their own cooking. For this reason they carry with them in the car a complete camping and cooking outfit, as well as picks, shovels, ropes, and even fire arms. The latter will be used mainly for the purpose of scaring off any too curious animals along the way, while the picks and shovels will be used to dig out of the few bad spots which will, of course, be encountered on the way. In addition to these the ladies have with them in the car plenty of rope and tackle, as well as long strips of canvas, which will be used along the way on the sandy roads, in order to give the wheels a purchase when the shifting sands become so bad that the tires will not grip. On the whole it is a most interesting party and car, and one of the best equipped, probably, that has ever left New York bound for Frisco.

All the way to Omaha the Chicago and Northwestern tracks were within a few feet of the future Lincoln Highway. The train started a southwestern course out of Vail, passing through Denison, Arion, Dow City, Dunlap, Woodbine, Logan, Missouri Valley, Loveland, Honey Creek, Crescent, and Council Bluffs, before heading up to the railroad bridge over the Missouri River into Omaha.

Had Alice been seated by a window on the right side of the coach, she would have seen the muddy tracks of the future Lincoln Highway—frequently filled water, as she rolled through western Iowa. She was riding along the Boyer River.

She would have crossed the Missouri River on the C&NW bridge, which according to UP railroad historian Donald R. Snoddy was about eight blocks south of the old vehicular bridge, which in turn was a block south of the present bridge.

She would have had a six-block walk, or a five-minute buggy ride, from the depot at 10th and Jackson Streets to the Rome Hotel, which stood at 16th and Jackson.

Collection of Gregory M. Franzwa

Postcard view of the Rome Hotel, 16th and Jackson Streets, Omaha.

Vail, Iowa, to Cheyenne, Wyoming

Alice had left the mired Maxwell in Vail, pop. 631, in 1915. After her return from Omaha on Wednesday, June 30, she probably drove to Denison, then turned to the northwest for three miles before the axle gave way. According to Mearl T. Luvaas, Denison's leading historian, Alice most likely would have stayed at the Hotel Denison.

Denison was a thriving community, with the 1915 *Road Guide* listing a population of 3,500. There were four other hotels, but Hotel Denison was the most expensive, at $2.00-$2.50 a night

Collection of Mearl T. Luvaas

This real-photo postcard of Hotel Denison was made about 1930.

Collection of Mearl T. Luvaas

Spittoons were placed at strategic sites in the lobby of Hotel Denison. This real photo postcard probably was made about the turn of the century. The "Ladie's Parlor," a similar real-photo card from the same collection (not shown), displayed no such amenities.

189

Alice probably would have left Denison on the street now identified as Avenue C, heading northwest. Crossing the tracks of the Illinois Central on the west edge of town, and then the adjacent Boyer, she would have reached the route of present US 59. Then she would have slanted off to the west a couple of miles from there onto Iowa 141. She didn't mention Charter Oak, which she drove through in eleven miles, nor that 141 turned north at Ute, six miles west of there. Mapleton, pop. 1,294 in the 1990 census, was eleven miles to the northwest; and Smithland, pop. 252 in 1990, was another nine miles farther to the northwest. Just west of Smithland, where 141 slants to the west, Iowa 982 leads northwest to Sioux City, and there Alice would cool her radiator for three agonizing days, waiting for the Midwest to dry up.

Collection of Gregory M. Franzwa

The West Hotel, Sioux City.

It was our good fortune to find Gary Sides, of Dakota City, Nebr., who solved all of our problems around Jackson, some thirteen miles from the Combination Bridge over the Missouri River at Sioux City. First, he knew that the only hotel in Jackson in 1909 was the Kennelly. He couldn't come up with a photo of the place, but he did find a plat of the town, dated 1911. He faxed it to us, with the site of the Kennelly encircled, on the south side of the Chicago, St. Paul, Minneapolis, and Omaha Railroad tracks.

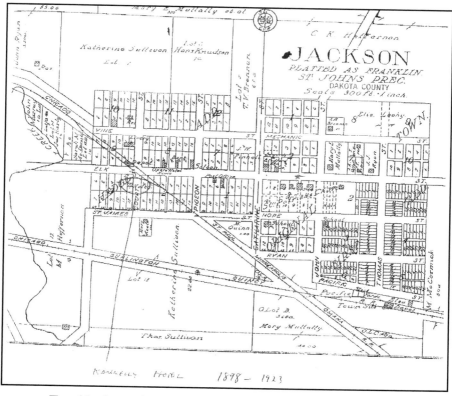

Two blocks to the east, on Elk Street (the main drag), is a building identified as a lumberyard. Then he faxed two photos, shown on the next page, looking west on Elk Street, both showing the lumberyard on the right. Alice's hotel would have been down the street, and a half-block to the left.

They were copied from an old newspaper, then faxed—thus the poor quality of reproduction.

Then Gary found a clip from the July 16, 1909, issue of the *Dakota City Eagle,* datelined July 9, some three days after Alice headed west from Sioux City:

Very heavy rains are daily occurrences in Jackson. On the bottom and low lands it is almost impossible for farmers to work in the fields. However,

the corn promises to be a fine stand, but wheat and oats are not so good. Fruit is in excellent condition. . . .

Mr. R. Buol drove his auto to Sioux City last Friday for a few days' visit. In taking a spin Sunday on the Nebraska side, his machine got stuck in the mud near Dakota City and at this writing he has not returned it to the protection of the home garage.

Gary describes the terrain ahead of Alice: "My father drove a truck for a number of years out of Denison, Iowa. The road from Denison to Sioux

City is higher and hilly, out of the mud. The road south to Blair or Omaha is flat and low (muddy). From Sioux City through Jackson and Homer, Nebr., the road is flat, then gets sort of hilly again."

The Maxwell plunged west, taking many left-right section-line turns to follow close to the route of future US 20 for about sixteen miles, to reach Allen (pop. 331 in 1990). Alice would have continued south for about thirty miles, but how she got through to Wisner is anybody's guess. There were dirt roads all the way, according to a 1925 plat of eastern Nebraska supplied by Gary. He was able to come up with a photograph of the Wisner Hotel as well as a 1915 newspaper photo of Wisner's main street.

The Wisner Hotel was a popular place to spend a night. The hotel was located on the north side of Avenue E and 10t Street. A vacant lot is now located there.

Collection of Gary Sides

Wisner *News Chronicle*

Alice's Drive

Finding the road that took Alice to Columbus was not easy, nor is it a certainty. Gary's over-the-road dad, Jerry Sides, speculated that dirt section-line roads would have been taken from Howells, which is on Nebr. 91. From there she would have driven west to Leigh, to spend the night.

We asked a close friend, Corrine Rickner, of Columbus, to help us out with Leigh, Nebr., where Alice spent Thursday night, July 8, in a hotel. She recommended we contact Esther Mohnsen, a retired schoolteacher who now lives in Leigh. Esther scrounged around and found this picture of the North-western, the only hotel in town.

Alice was driving on the dirt road that became NE 91, about a mile north of Leigh. She turned south on Main Street, and drove the Maxwell into a livery stable as she neared the hotel.

Consulting Mapquest on the web, we found a cemetery on the map of Creston, but it was some six miles northwest of town—that couldn't be the place where Alice turned south to drive to Columbus. Corrine knew there was a cemetery near the east edge of Creston, and she knew that the paved Monastery Road led south from there to Columbus. Jerry Sides verified this. It was in Columbus where Alice's battles with mud were almost over, and where her path to San Francisco coincided with the Lincoln Highway of 1913-28.

Alice now followed the left bank of the broad Platte River, as did the covered wagon pioneers of sixty years earlier. She drove through the delightful little towns of Duncan, Silver Creek, Clarks, Central City, and Chapman.

Alice left no clue about her hotel during the three-night stay in Grand Island. It could have been the Palmer House—the postcard image here was postmarked August 13, 1900, and it was among the five listed in the 1915 *Road Guide*—$2 to $3 a night.

Palmer House, Grand Island, NE

The Union Pacific followed along the north bank of the Platte, but the dirt roads certainly did not. The roads west were section-line roads along here. The women passed through many little towns, just as do those who follow the old Lincoln Highway today—Alda, Wood River, Shelton, Gibbon, and finally Kearney—across the river from historic Fort Kearny. There the Platte changed course, from southwest to northwest, and the Maxwell continued its left-right-left-right passage through Odessa and Elm Creek to Overton, where the travelers spent the night of July 12, 1909.

As they neared Gothenburg, Nebr., they would have seen a long wood bridge leading south across the Platte. That was a lifesaver to later Lincoln Highway travelers, who crossed the river there and took the "Gothenburg Stairstep"—more left-right roads, to North Platte. Deep sand on the north bank mandated this. The road to the south was opened by travelers on the

Special Collections, University of Michigan Library

*Described as "The Old Buffalo Trail near Kearney, Nebr.," this photo
is probably of the road traveled by the Maxwell in 1909.*

Gregory M. Franzwa

*The sort of dirt road Alice encountered in central Nebraska is illus-
trated in this 1996 photograph of the 1913 Lincoln Highway, just west of
Richland.*

Oregon-California Trail, as well as the later Overland Stage.

Curiously, Alice doesn't mention that old bridge, which is long gone. But there still is a path through the woods, exiting from the south side to the Stairstep. When entering North Platte, she would have crossed water on a long bridge over the South Platte, then the North Platte. The split between the two branches of the river was a mile or two east of the bridge.

Collection of Gregory M. Franzwa

The old Platte Bridge, Gothenburg, Nebraska, photographed about 1910.

The Maxwell chugged west through Hershey, Sutherland, Paxton, and Roscoe, before stopping in Ogallala for the night of July 13. But where?

We called the Ogallala Chamber of Commerce for help, and Cindy Ford answered the phone. That was our lucky day. We wanted to find Alice's hotel, and that was a problem that took Cindy *days* to solve. She hung in there and got the job done.

There are three hotels listed in the 1915 *Road Guide*—the Hollingsworth, Martin, and Barrett. Cindy searched the *Keith County News* for June, July, and August, 1909, and found no mention of any Ogallala hotels, or of Alice Ramsey. She found two hotels south of the tracks, which

Alice's Drive

Gregory M. Franzwa

Alice's road emerged from the south end of the Platte Bridge right here.

burned in 1912. "One may have been Ogallala House, considered pretty fancy."

More research revealed that the Ogallala House actually burned in 1884. Turned out to be a house of ill repute, managed by Mrs. H. Gast, "Madame."

On February 11, 1909, the *Keith County News* reported that "The Barrett house has fallen into good hands again. O. C. Cross, the present proprietor, is setting a first class table and furnishes his guests with good clean beds. His business is steadily growing and by close attention to business he will make this house one of the paying institutions of Ogallala."

The March 4 edition of the paper: "Our hotels are enjoying a good run of business, both being crowded. The Hotel Martin has always enjoyed a good business and the Barrett Hotel under its new management is coming to

Had Alice taken the north bank route to North Platte, this is the sort f path she would have had to follow.

ie front and enjoying a good run."

Cindy's conclusions: "The Martin House was next to or maybe icluded in the G.A.R. Hall and Martin Pool Hall. It was struck by lightning n May 15, 1913, and burned. Chance are pretty good that Alice and her ssociates did *not* stay here.

"The Barrett House went through several owners and was listed for nt again in April 1910. It burned in September 1910 in a block fire that ok out several businesses on South Spruce Street. I am *speculating* that it the area between US 30 and the Union Pacific tracks, where the current uenz Drug is located."

Evidently the target hotel was the Barrett. No photo has surfaced.

During her search, Cindy came across an article about the Rollie lann murder. "I was really surprised that the Keith County sheriff stopped lice Ramsey. The woman whose husband committed the crime told the ithorities in Denver that her husband did it. She was very frightened of m, thinking that he might do her in, too. The law rewarded her by giving r thirty-nine years in the state pen with no parole, and her husband got life. hink she got a bad deal. Could it be that Alice was delayed because they ere exhuming the body of Rollie Mann? He was buried around Roscoe, on the north side of the Platte."

Our travelers evidently were unaware of it, but they were now in western Nebraska's sand hills, mud problems having been replaced by sand problems.

Alice drove west from Ogallala, over or near the route of present U.S. 30. After passing Brule she could have looked to the left to see the old Lower California Crossing of the South Platte, taken by the covered wagons heading to Oregon. Looking to the right she could have seen the deep scars of the Oregon-California Trail leading up California Hill. But she probably did neither, fighting the steering wheel through the sandy track straight through the towns of Big Spring, Chappell, Sidney, Potter, Dix, and Kimball, to Bushnell.

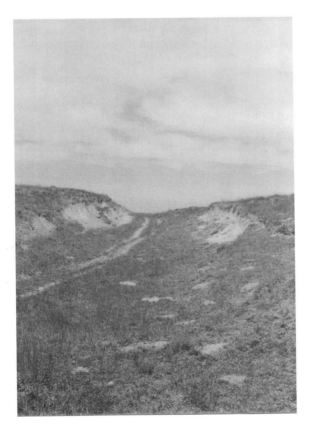

The great swale of the Oregon-California Trail, passing over California Hill near Brule, Nebr., was photographed in 1997.
Gregory M. Franzwa

Those who would like to see the track of the 1913 Lincoln Highway, the exact path taken by Alice four years earlier, could leave US 30 in Bushnell, turn back to the east on the north side of the highway, driving about a mile to the end of the access road at the Bushnell Cemetery. Then if they turn right and look east over the fence and into the pasture, they can see the tracks, plain as day, and appearing much as they would have in 1909.

Pine Bluffs, Wyoming, was only ten miles west of Bushnell, and from there the travelers would have taken unimproved roads, probably two-tracks, through Egbert, Burns, Durham, and Archer, before entering Cheyenne on 16th Street.

Gregory M. Franzwa

The Maxwell's tires would have helped make these scars through the prairie east of Bushnell, Nebraska.

Cheyenne to Opal, Wyoming

Alice motored past the Union Pacific depot on her left, then as now the most magnificent edifice on the railroad. Built in 1886-87, the structure has been completely restored and stands more beautiful than ever along Lincolnway.

Neg. #4659, Wyoming State Archives
Cheyenne's Union Station was photographed in the early 1930s.

Just past the railroad station Alice crossed Capitol Avenue, pulled alongside the long portico in front of Cheyenne's Inter-Ocean Hotel, leaned to the left and snapped the switch on the coil box to kill the engine. The women were home for the next thirty-six hours. Randy Wagner, past-president

Wyoming State Archives

of today's Lincoln Highway Association and one of Wyoming's leading historians, wrote that the Inter-Ocean was built in 1873 and burned shortly after Alice's visit, killing six. The site is now occupied by the long-vacant Hynds Building. The historic buildings in the western part of that block were gutted by fire in December 2004.

The Maxwellites lingered a day in the Wild West town of Cheyenne and headed west on Friday, July 16, 1909. Her book carries a photograph, way out of order, of the settlement of Granite Canyon, just thirteen miles west of Cheyenne.

Wyoming Department of Transportation

This photograph of Granite Canyon was taken probably a decade after Alice took the shot in her book, from almost the same angle. It shows a much-improved road.

Exposed outcrops of the Sherman granite found here provided the best ballast on the Union Pacific Railroad, along with a fine aggregate for

many miles of Wyoming's early Lincoln Highway. Furthermore, an artesian
well there supplied much of the sparkling, clear water served on the railroad's
dining cars.

(Alice wrote in her diary almost every day, but arranged her photo
graphs more than a half-century later—it is understandable how some pictures
could be out of order.)

By stopping (illegally) on the I-80 overpass sixteen miles west of
Cheyenne, one can see the old two-track taken by the travelers as it comes
from the southeast, up to the point where the embankment of the interstate
truncated it. That road was once the great Lincoln Highway—now just a
faint path through the High Desert.

Today's I-80 does a very peculiar thing about thirty-three miles west
of Cheyenne. Travelers in the westbound lanes may slant off *to the left* into
a roadside picnic area and read all about an old gnarled limber pine growing
out of a crevice in a granite boulder—"Tree Rock." Randy Wagner, not only
a fine historian but a talented journalist as well, wrote the text for the infor
mation panels next to the venerable old tree.

Alice drove to the south of the tree, on the 1868 right-of-way
abandoned by the Union Pacific just eight years earlier—the same path taken
by the Lincoln Highway in 1913. It was just sand then. It is just sand now.
But it coursed right by the Ames Monument, shown in this real-photo postcard.

Collection of Gregory M. Franzwa

The pyramid, sixty feet high, commemorated Oakes and Oliver Ames. Oliver was the third president of Union Pacific and director of Crédit Mobilier, set up to finance construction of the railroad. Oakes, Oliver's brother, served in the U.S. Congress, promoting sweetheart legislation for the railroad. Alice passed within yards of it in 1909, but about a mile away from it on her later trips on the Lincoln Highway, US 30, and I-80.

Driving north of Laramie Alice would have passed through the hamlets of Howell (totally disappeared today), Wyoming (also gone), Bosler (two or three abandoned buildings left), Lookout (gone), and Harper (also gone), until arriving in Rock River.

LINCOLN HIGHWAY ENTERING ROCK RIVER, WYOMING

Collection of Brian Butko

Real-photo postcard of the Lincoln Highway entering Rock River from the south. Chances are Alice Ramsey took the same graded dirt road into the town.

The road through Medicine Bow is little changed from Alice's day. She left the paved US 30 at the now-restored Virginian Hotel, turned south to cross the Union Pacific tracks, then west again. The Lincoln Highway followed the same track in 1913. The town had a population of 150 in 1915; 274 in the 2000 census.

Rock River's Lincoln Hotel still stands. Alice Ramsey and her companions may have spent the night of July 16, 1909, in this building. The only hotel listed in the 1915 Road Guide *was the Phelan, which might not have been this structure. The town had 200 inhabitants in 1915.*

Alice's road north of Rock River probably didn't look nearly as good as it did in this 1996 view.

Wyoming State Archives

The view to the south across the Union Pacific tracks in Medicine Bow is shown here. The road turned to the right in front of the general store. Local lore says that Owen Wister slept one night on the counter of the little building to the left.

Collection of Gregory M. Franzwa

A real-photo postcard of the Virginian Hotel in Medicine Bow. Built in 1911 and named for Owen Wister's famed 1902 novel, it's still a wonderful place to dine and spend a night.

Fort Fred Steele was built in 1868 to protect the Union Pacific Railroad against Indian depredations. It was deactivated in 1886 and is now a Wyoming State Historic Site. The Lincoln Highway was moved alongside US 30 in the late 1930s.

Collection of Gregory M. Franzwa

Postcard of a Union Pacific train crossing the North Platte River at Fort Steele.

The 1915 *Road Guide* listed three hotels in Rawlins—the Ferris, the Abbott, and the Cottage. There were two garages and gasoline was 25¢ a gallon. The local speed limit of 12 mph was not enforced.

Alice took a long drive on July 18, passing through Creston, Wamsutter, Tipton, and Table Rock. Had she looked south there she would have seen the spectacular Table Rock, about ten miles to the south. She would have continued through the bitter Red Desert to Point of Rocks, and had she looked at the hillside across the tracks to the south she would have seen the Point of Rocks Overland Stage Station. The buildings have now been restored.

Then she would have driven through the hamlet of Thayer Junction, and in another eighteen miles, the bustling city of Rock Springs.

Rock Springs boasted a population of 7,500 in the 1915 *Road Guide*. Gas was 23¢ and the town enforced its speed limit of 8 mph. The coal mining industry supported 3,000 families, and by 1915 there were more than 100 automobiles on the streets.

208

The twin westbound lanes of I-80 are shown climbing Cherokee Hill, nineteen miles west of Rawlins. This 1996 photo also shows the line of the gravel Lincoln Highway just to the right. It was dirt, not gravel, when Alice took it.

Gregory M. Franzwa

Wyoming Department of Transportation

This was US 30 between Rawlins and Rock Springs, in the late 1920s.

209

The restored Point of Rocks Overland Stage Station, southeast of Point of Rocks, Wyoming.

Continuing west, the Maxwell would have passed through spectacular town of Green River, where the Lincoln Highway was squeezed between the historic stream and the towering formations on the right. Then the travelers would have arrived in the town of Granger.

The Lincoln Highway turned south in Granger, heading for Fort Bridger, but Alice was advised to continue northwest through Moxa and Nutria, to arrive at Opal, some thirty miles west of Granger. Opal's population in 2000 was listed at 101—it probably was considerably larger in 1909.

Karen Rennells feels this photo of Opal was taken about 1899. One of these structures could have been the hotel occupied by Alice Ramsey and her friends. And, of course, the bedbugs.

Karen Buck Rennells, a whiz on the Oregon-California Trail, lives on the Buck Ranch south of LaBarge, Wyo. She advises that in 1899 Opal (pronounced o-PAL, by the way) had two hotels. One became the Opal Merc, which is still standing. "It's a brick building and you can still see 'HOTEL' on the side." The top floor of that building was a hotel of sorts.

However, Karen feels that Alice stayed in the Opal Hotel, not on the top floor of the Merc.

Opal, Wyoming, to Reno, Nevada

The later Lincoln Highway turned southwest in Granger on what became US 30S, to historic Fort Bridger, to enter Evanston. Alice, for whatever reason, continued on what became US 30N (and later just plain US 30). She did not drive into Kemmerer—US 30N turned north in Oakley, but Alice turned south there, following what became US 189 to a Y in the road just north of the Uinta County line. The left road led to Carter and Lyman; the right branch, (US 189) proceeds south to link up with I-80 some thirteen miles east of Evanston.

Alice turned half-right at the Y—no question about that—but she didn't follow the road designated today as US 189. The road she took is no longer on the maps, not even Mapquest. She took a bee-line drive over a network of faint two-tracks toward Evanston, and when she was about a mile north of town she turned due south, evidently right on the route of present Wyo.89.

Alice's route from there can be followed only a short distance from the *Blue Books*. She would have continued south on 89, now also Painter Lane, across Bear River, crossing into the Evanston business district.

After crossing the Bear River, today's drivers should turn right on Front Street for a few blocks to Harrison Street, and then turning left there, drive up the hill to the west edge of Evanston. There the driver should turn right onto Wasatch. That's the route of the Lincoln Highway.

Alice would have followed Wasatch for a short distance, then crossed the tracks to the north, but that leads to a private ranch today, with locked gates. So today's drivers should simply proceed west on Wasatch to the point where the road surface changes from blacktop to gravel. That is the Utah state line.

There once was a railroad station there, but no longer. Five miles ahead was the town of Wasatch, pop. 10 in 1915; pop. 0 in 2000. Thirteen miles into Utah is Castle Rock, pop. 20 in 1915; pop. 0 in 2000. Emory Station is eight miles ahead, where there are three or four trees—even the old section house is gone. But the Lincoln Highway went all along here—the pavement is still up on the bench, next to the cliffs to the north. Alice's road was sometimes there, sometimes down below, where faint two-tracks may be seen from time to time.

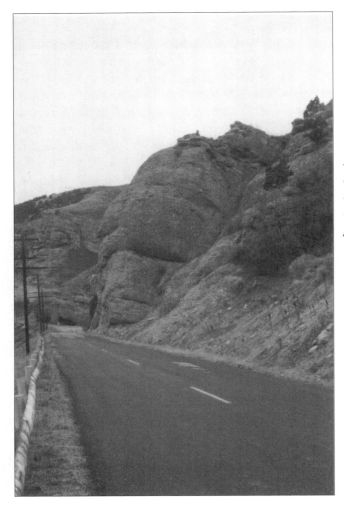

The Lincoln Highway near Baskin Siding, 4.5 miles west of Emory Station, was photographed in 1999.

Gregory M. Franzwa

About thirty miles into Utah Alice passed a fork to the left and proceeded a half-mile ahead to arrive at the town of Echo, where Frank Cattelan maintains the Echo Café. The Lincoln Highway of 1915 turned left at the fork, to enter Salt Lake City via Coalville and Parleys Canyon. But in 1913, responding to pressure from the governor of Utah, the highway was routed down Weber Canyon—the very route taken by Alice four years earlier.

Alice was a bit off in her estimation of the height of the walls of Devil's Slide. They are more like thirty feet high.

Devil's Slide was photographed from the turnout off the west-bound lanes of I-84. The Union Pacific tracks, the rushing Weber River, and a service road are at the base of the formation.
Gregory M. Franzwa

Driving north, the Maxwell would have threaded its way through Devil's Gate, a few miles west of Devil's Slide, and approached Ogden. She would not have entered Ogden, however, and instead turned south past Uinta, following close to SR 126 through the towns of Clearfield, Layton, then 106

213

through Kaysville, Farmington, Centerville, and on US 89 through Bountiful. Salt Lake City would have been entered from the north on N 2nd West, and Alice would have turned east on South Temple Street. Chances are she would have turned right on Main Street and driven right to the post office, which was located between Third and Fourth on the south side of Main. The adventurers spent the next several nights at the Knutsford Hotel, which was located on the northeast corner of State Street and 300 South.

Alice and her companions left the Mormon capital on Saturday, July 24. They rode south to 21st Street, either on Main or State Street. They would have turned right there—the same way they had taken when they went to Saltaire.

The mining company mentioned would have been present Kennecott, whose stacks still tower above the south shore of the Great Salt Lake. Alice's route, as well as the later Lincoln Highway, passed right through the grounds of the company, some of the path obscured now by tailings of the copper company.

Past present Lake Point they would have marveled at the expanse of the Great Salt Lake, and in a mile or two would have passed imposing Adobe Rock—a landmark since the days of the covered wagons heading to California.

Gregory M. Franzwa

Adobe Rock

Past Adobe Rock the Maxwell would have been on SR 138 through Grantsville, then on west to round the northern tip of the Stansbury Mountains. There 138 turns south. Today's travelers should continue west for less than a mile, to turn south on the Skull Valley Road. Driving for just a few dozen yards, a dirt road on the left can be taken back to the east, to arrive at Big Spring, a popular campground of the emigrants, including the Donner Party. And just south of the pond is the straight-as-a-string Lincoln Highway, a dirt path only wide enough for one narrow car. That is the original Skull Valley Road, the drive taken by Alice Ramsey in 1909.

Gregory M. Franzwa

Alice Ramsey pointed her Maxwell south on the Skull Valley Road from Big Spring to Orr's Ranch.

The Orr Ranch was established in 1890, and Shirley Orr Andrus, granddaughter of the founder, lives there to this day. She and her husband, Dennis Andrus, still offer hospitality to travelers on the 1913 route of the Lincoln Highway. Her parents, William and Pearl, probably welcomed Alice and her friends when they limped in on July 24, 1909. The axle repair took place beneath a lean-to next to the log cabin, where Pearl prepared meals for early travelers, and that cabin stands to this day, maintained with pride by Dennis and Shirley.

Gregory M. Franzwa

The Lincoln Highway cabin on Orr's Ranch

Special Collections, University of Michigan Library

West of Orr's Ranch, deep ruts and grinding hills marked the Cedar Mountain cutoff, shown here in 1916.

The Cedar Mountain cutoff, leading to today's Dugway Proving Grounds, begins only a mile southwest of Orr's Ranch. It's a good bet that the Maxwell avoided this hilly route.

Alice would have entered the present Dugway Proving Grounds, a federal testing facility, north of present English Village. Visitors to DPG are allowed today, with permission, but are still greeted by a phalanx of uniformed soldiers brandishing automatic weapons, just in case things don't look right. Alice's path would have been about a mile south of present Stark Road, and past Little Granite Mountain she probably would have stopped at County Well. That site has absolutely disappeared from the face of the earth.

In a few yards she would have arrived at Government Creek, usually a dry wash but sometimes filled with rushing water. A little bridge there dates to about 1900, and it's still there, a photographic target for today's Lincoln Highway travelers. An interpretive panel informs visitors that the structure is on the National Register of Historic Places.

Gregory M. Franzwa

The bridge over Government Creek on the Dugway Proving Grounds was photographed in 1994.

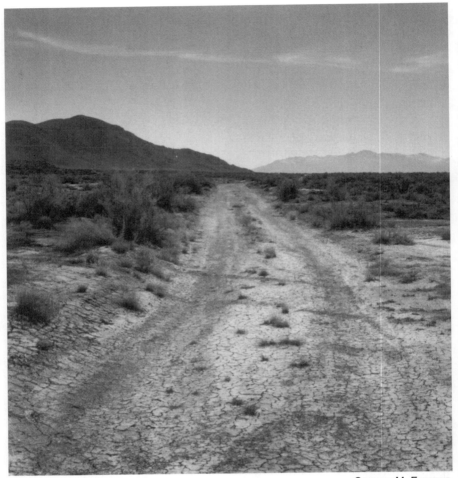

Gregory M. Franzwa

Enroute to Fish Springs, the wheels of the Maxwell DA rolled over this portion of the future Lincoln Highway on Saturday, July 24, 1909.

Fish Springs, on the Pony Express route, is south of Dugway. Now a National Wildlife Reserve, it was once the headquarters of John J. Thomas. After 1913, Thomas made a good living hauling Lincoln Highway travelers out of the mud.

John J. Thomas and his Model T Ford. Standing at six feet two, he posed before his main ranch building, an Overland Stage station built about 1862.

Sheridan's Ranch, Ibapah, had no "hotel" in 1909, but there were a few log cabins on the property, one or more of which might have been for rent.

Alice Ramsey and her companions may have stayed in one of these log cabins at Sheridan's Ranch on July 29, 1909.

Alice didn't mention the Tippett Ranch when she drove by it, some twenty miles west of the Utah/Nevada line. She probably stopped there, for it was a regular C-store for travelers. The sign in front of the building listed the services—gas, oil, post office, general merchandise, groceries, meals, rooms, dry goods, and AAA services.

Special Collections, University of Michigan Library

Tippett Ranch looked like this in the late 1920s. It has been abandoned for a half-century.

Where did Alice take the wrong turn? Probably at the south end of Spring Valley, but possibly right at "Stonehouse."

Gregory M. Franzwa

A 2003 view of Stonehouse, overlooking Spring Valley

Ely boasted six hotels in 1915. The women probably stayed at the Northern. The building burned in the 1960s, and the site is now a vacant lot. This ad appeared in the 1923 *Blue Book:*

Northern Hotel	ROOMS SINGLE AND EN SUITE
	RATES { $1.00 Per Day & Up Without Bath / $2.00 Per Day & Up With Bath
Ely, Nevada	STEAM HEATED THROUGHOUT

East Ely Railroad Museum
Ely's Northern Hotel, photographed in the early 1920s.

The 1923 *Blue Book* guides travelers south to Hamilton, then returns them back north before resuming a westerly course. Alice did no such thing, plowing directly west and then north to Eureka.

In 1915 Eureka boasted a population of 785, down quite a bit since the Maxwell drove through in 1909. She arrived there on Saturday night, July 31. Brown's Hotel is next to Eureka's Opera House, a stunning restoration which has given new life to the old town.

221

Eureka's dusty main street was photographed in 1915.

Gregory M. Franzwa

Brown's Hotel, left, and the Eureka Opera House in 1996.

Holden Collection, Lincoln Highway Association

The Opera House is at the far right, and Brown's Hotel is next to it.

Alice would have driven through the heart of Austin on her way to the Walsh Ranch, past the International Hotel in the center of town. The International was erected in Virginia City, Nevada, in 1859, and dismantled and moved to Austin three years later. It has been in business ever since—no longer a hotel but a busy restaurant today.

Austin's International Hotel today
Gregory M. Franzwa

223

Alice was lavish in her praise of the engine in the DA, and it must have been wonderful indeed. The old grades leading up to New Pass, west of Austin, were sometimes in excess of fifteen percent. Yet, the little car evidently didn't falter as it pulled the four women over the 6,348-foot summit.

The road gets increasingly sandier to the west. The travelers probably were advised to leave the road that became the Lincoln Highway, in order to avoid the Four-mile and Eight-mile Flats, known together as the Fallon Flats.

Special Collections, University of Michigan Library

Heavy ore wagons ripped up the sandy road east of Fallon. This photo was made in 1916, but it was several years after that before the road could be passed safely.

Special Collections, University of Michigan Library

This western Nevada photograph was made in 1915, as the car on the left was about to enter the Fallon Flats.

Rawhide was a good twenty-five mile detour to the south of the main road. The town was already in decline when Alice stopped on Monday night, August 2, 1909. A succession of fires leveled the town, and it was never rebuilt.

The women would have proceeded west from Rawhide on August 3, to a point just south of Fallon, and then taken a series of two-tracks north to the town.

When they crossed the Truckee River on a primitive bridge in Wadsworth, they were very near the spot where tens of thousands of covered wagons crossed that same river some sixty years earlier.

Reno to the Golden Gate

From Wadsworth, Alice would have followed the emigrant road up the Truckee Canyon, on or very near the route of today's I-80, entering Sparks on today's B Avenue. Sparks was a charming little town in 1909, and it is a charming little city today. The population of 2,500 had grown to 3,238 by 1925, and mushroomed to more than 66,000 people today.

B Avenue eventually became Fourth Street in Reno. Its population was only 12,000 in 1915, and nine years later had picked up a net of sixteen people. Today? 183,000. There were more than a dozen hotels in Reno in 1915, but one dominated—the Riverside. Rates were $2.50 to $4.

Gregory M. Franzwa

Reno's Riverside Hotel today

225

The Riverside still stands on the south bank of the Truckee, but now serves low-income residents. The travelers turned left when they arrived at Reno's Virginia Street, crossed the Truckee, and pulled up in front of the hotel. Chances are there would have been plenty of glitter at the midnight hour across the river, but South Virginia would have been fairly dark when Alice killed the engine, and snuffed out the headlights and the oil lamps on the Maxwell.

To get to Carson City today one needs only to drive south on Virginia Street for thirty miles. That road, US 385, proceeds along the west shore of shallow Washoe Lake. Not quite so easy in Alice's day. There were jogs and several forks along the way, and the roads were so primitive that one way looked as bad as the other. They probably would have noticed the elegant 1863 Bowers mansion on the west side of the road about sixteen miles south of town. (Bowers was a silver king who struck it rich in nearby Virginia City.)

By the early 1920s Reno was Nevada's biggest city by far, and tiny Carson City was the state capital. A great combination for road building, so the two cities were linked by concrete in the early 1920s.

Chasing Alice

The travelers now were on what became the Pioneer Branch of the Lincoln Highway, 1913-20. The final route of the Pioneer Branch started a few miles west of Fallon, where present US 50 slants to the southwest as 50A, continuing to Reno. The US 50 route was made official in 1920, but until then the Pioneer Branch started at Fourth and Virginia in Reno.

Alice would have turned right in Carson City on King Street, at the state capitol, and followed it to the west. Soon it became the Kings Canyon Road, leading a dozen miles south to Spooner Summit. People who want to take that road today are in for either a thrill or a disaster, depending upon whether they are driving a 2WD or a 4WD vehicle. In either event, the Carson Ranger District of the US Forest Service should be contacted about road conditions before venturing onto that narrow, boulder-strewn road. Their number: 775/882-2766.

Gregory M. Franzwa

The Kings Canyon Road, known in later years as the Ostermann Grade, is shown here as a thin line, high in the Sierra Nevada, going from right to left.

It takes about three hours to make the twelve-mile drive on the Kings

227

Canyon Road. Swifts Station stood at the summit, and although Alice doesn't mention it, she must have noticed some vestiges of a decaying civilization up there. It once sported a hotel, cabins, a barn, and probably some sort of food service. Nothing remains at the site today but scatter.

Collection of Joe Nardone

This remarkable photograph of Swifts Station was taken about 1864, when the Kings Canyon Road was a route across the mountains for freight wagons.

Three miles after leaving Glenbrook the women would have squeezed around Cave Rock on a narrow trestle high above Lake Tahoe—they could not have reached the lakeshore any other way. The Kings Canyon Road must have inured the women to breath-catching situations, as there is no mention of Cave Rock in Alice's narrative.

The narrow ledge shown in this 1915 view outside Cave Rock was shored up with a trestle. The rock approaches are still there. Tunnels were later drilled through the rock and the route over the trestle was closed.

After the high deserts of Wyoming and the dense forests of western Nevada, Alice was euphoric about the scenery from Lake Tahoe down the Sierra slopes.

This street, on the south shore of Lake Tahoe, is named "Lincoln Highway."

Gregory M. Franzwa

Along the road to Placerville, which is US 50 today, the Maxwell was cruising at 10-15 mph some ten to twenty miles north of the road that carried miners by the hundreds of thousands into California during the gold rush of 1849-59. They were traveling at the rate of three to four miles an hour. That is also the road that carried discharged members of the Mormon Battalion from the diggings to their yet-unseen homes in Great Salt Lake City. (The Mormons actually opened the Carson Road, from west to east, in 1848.) The Maxwell would have passed the intersection of present CA 49, one of the most historic roads in the West—connecting such legendary gold towns of Coloma, Sutter Creek, Amador, Murphys, and Angels Camp.

There were three hotels in Placerville in 1909, but Alice's book does not say where they stayed the night of Thursday, August 5.

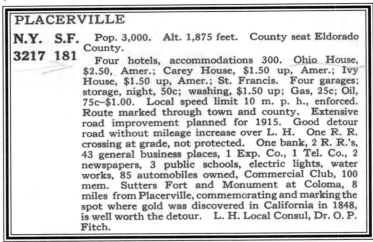

PLACERVILLE

N.Y. S.F. Pop. 3,000. Alt. 1,875 feet. County seat Eldorado County.
3217 181 Four hotels, accommodations 300. Ohio House, $2.50, Amer.; Carey House, $1.50 up, Amer.; Ivy House, $1.50 up, Amer.; St. Francis. Four garages; storage, night, 50c; washing, $1.50 up; Gas, 25c; Oil, 75c–$1.00. Local speed limit 10 m. p. h., enforced. Route marked through town and county. Extensive road improvement planned for 1915. Good detour road without mileage increase over L. H. One R. R. crossing at grade, not protected. One bank, 2 R. R.'s, 43 general business places, 1 Exp. Co., 1 Tel. Co., 2 newspapers, 3 public schools, electric lights, water works, 85 automobiles owned, Commercial Club, 100 mem. Sutters Fort and Monument at Coloma, 8 miles from Placerville, commemorating and marking the spot where gold was discovered in California in 1848, is well worth the detour. L. H. Local Consul, Dr. O. P. Fitch.

Complete Official Road Guide of the Lincoln Highway, 1915

It's likely that Alice and her friends stayed at the Ohio House in Placerville.

The travelers were excited now—they were on the home stretch. Alice can be excused for leaving out details of their passage from Placerville— even Sacramento, the California capital, was unmentioned. They would have turned south there on present CA 99, to drive through Galt to Stockton. There they would have turned west near the route of present I-205, through the towns of Tracy and Livermore, finally reaching Hayward, for their last night on the road to San Francisco.

The 1915 *Road Guide* four hotels for Hayward, the most elegant being Hayward's, built in late 1800s. It burned in 1922.

Hayward Area Historical Society

Alice Ramsey may have spent her last night on the road in the large Hayward's Hotel, on Mission Blvd.

A number of ferry boats were crossing the bay in 1909, most of them coal burners. They tied up at the slips at the Ferry Building.

Collection of Gregory M. Franzwa

The travelers would have driven the Maxwell onto a boat such as the one approaching from the right, landing at San Francisco's Ferry Building. The structure has been completely restored.

The parade of Maxwells would have met Alice's daughty little DA at the Ferry Building, escorting her and her companions proudly down Market Street, probably for a mile and a half, possibly slanting off to the right onto Grove. The St. James was three blocks to the west and a block to the right, at Fulton and Van Ness. Construction was about to begin on San Francisco's City Hall, on the east side of Van Ness. The original city hall was destroyed by the earthquake of 1906. We can thank George L. Clark of San Francisco for his expertise in finding Alice's hotel and deducing her route.

The San Francisco press responded dutifully to J.D.'s handouts. Clark pulled this clip from the *San Francisco Chronicle* dated Sunday, August 8:

PRETTY WOMEN MOTORISTS ARRIVE AFTER TRIP ACROSS THE CONTINENT
Mrs. Ramsey Here
In Maxwell
Car

Forty-Two Hundred Miles Over
All Kinds of Roads and
Mountains.

By W. H. B. Fowler.

As remarkable an automobile trip as any ever undertaken in this country was completed yesterday, when Mrs. John R. Ramsey of Hackensack, N. J., accompanied by three women companions, drove her Maxwell car up Market street after a run across the Continent that logged about 4200 miles. Just two days less than two months was taken for the journey. The record across the continent of course, is much faster than that, but it has been made by men out for speed. Even at that few have attempted the long and strenuous journey, and the feat of Mrs. Ramsey and her companions, under the circumstances becomes all the more remarkable.

As charming a young person as one might wish to meet is this long-distance motorist. Her age, so it is stated, is 22 years, and there is no reason at all to doubt it. She is perhaps the last person in the world that one would expect to find piloting an automobile across the continent with none but three women companions, some hardly older than herself. . . .

The reporter then quoted Alice about the Iowa roads, but she was lavish in her praise of the scenery of Nebraska, Wyoming, and Nevada.

"I am really surprised that the trip has been so easy," she added. Then she let J.D. get in some licks for his employer—"This is due, of course, in a measure, to the fact that the car has stood up under some pretty hard jolting, and has not caused a bit of trouble since we left New York. Pretty nearly everything but the ditches we took on high, and in spite of the shaking the car has had I have yet to find anything even loosened."

The reporter added: "Mrs. Ramsey and her companions were the guests at luncheon yesterday of the Maxwell-Briscoe Pacific Company, and last evening they were entertained at dinner by E. A. Kelley of the Splitdorf Magneto Company at the St. James Hotel."

Splitdorf got in some licks in a companion story: "We had our Splitdorf magneto and spark plugs on the Maxwell car used by Mrs. Ramsey," said a company spokesman.

The *Examiner* story on the same day was much shorter, and contained considerably less baloney.

There was a similar story in the *San Francisco Call*, accompanied by a paid ad, *right*.

Alice's three companions stayed in San Francisco for a few days of sightseeing, but Alice, who had been away from Bone and her baby for two

233

months, boarded the Southern Pacific for home. And obscurity for half a century. It was in the 1960s that the world rediscovered Alice Ramsey and gave her the honors she so richly deserved.

Acknowledgments

Although Alice Ramsey wrote the best part of this book, I wrote most of it, and like my other nineteen, this one is heavily dependent upon people who have dug up pertinent information for our readers.

I'll start with the dedicatees—Jim Powell and Jim Ranniger. Powell dug into that route from Manhattan to Albany with vigor, even to the extent that he drove most of it. He supplied an enormous amount of primary materials on the Albany Post Road, including a very important 1905 book, plus a 1910 driving guide.

Jim Ranniger supplied a mint first edition of Alice Ramsey's *Veil, Duster, and Tire Iron*, and it was from that book that all Alice's pictures were copied. We tried for the originals, but the rights asked by the Detroit Public Library exceeded $7,000, with no opportunity for negotiation. Ramsey family members did not respond to our pleas for more information.

So here, in alphabetical order, are the names of the folks who gave so willingly of their time and expertise to make this book meaningful to the readers:

Larry Adams, of Boone, Iowa, remembered that the Northwestern Hotel was housed in Boone's Chicago and Northwestern Railroad depot, and even remembered when it was torn down.

Matt Anderson, with the Sioux City Museum, dug into his archives and found where Alice stayed waiting for Iowa's mud to dry up.

Jay Banta supplied the photo of John J. Thomas, of Fish Springs, Utah.

Van and Bev Becker, who performed that magnificent piece of research on Mechanicsville, Iowa, also filled us in on the Montrose Hotel in Cedar Rapids.

The folks at the Bergen County Historical Society, in New Jersey, supplied some data about John R. Ramsey.

Norma J. Berns, Carroll, Iowa, gave us the information on the Burke Hotel.

Virginia Bowers, the town historian for Albany, New York, worked hard to help us find Alice's route across the Hudson and through her city.

George L. Clark dropped everything and rushed to San Francisco City Library to dig out the microfilms of three daily newspapers, and search out information about the St. James Hotel.

Albert Dib, city historian for Hackensack, braved near blizzard conditions to track down information about Alice's life in that city.

Cindy Ford refused to give up when, day after day, she ran into blind alleys in the search for the hotel used by Alice Ramsey in Ogallala, Nebr. She not only found it, but information about the murder Alice mentioned as well.

Annette Fortin, resistrar of The Hudson River Museum in Yonkers, was very helpful in my search for Alice's route through her city.

Bob Gingerich, former mayor of Rochelle, Ill., was able to consult an amazing memory and come up with the name of Alice's hotel in that city.

Eileen M. Hayden, head of the Dutchess County Historical Society in Poughkeepsie, gave me a lot of information about the first night's stay of the expedition.

Candace Franzwa Johnson was helpful in my depiction of the Upper West Side of New York City in 1909.

Her daughter, New York attorney Sarah Johnson, looked at 1930 Broadway and provided the illustration of what is there today.

Ormie King knows more about Auburn, New York, than any man alive and is eager to share his knowledge with folks like me.

Sarah Kozma, with the Anondaga Historical Association in Syracuse, provided the information about that beautiful New York town on Alice's route.

We can thank Chuck Lanham for digging out the picture of Cheyenne's Inter-Ocean Hotel.

Dr. Richard Lenk, of Paramus, N.J., is Bergen County's most noted historian, and through him we learned where the Ramseys lived in Hackensack.

It was Bob Lichty, incoming president of the Lincoln Highway

Acknowledgments

Association and antique automobile whiz, who gave me some clues about finding Richard Anderson, the restorer of the Maxwell DA.

Almost every little town has a crack historian, and Mearl Luvaas fills that bill for Denison, Iowa. He knew where Alice stayed, where the Maxwell broke down, and how she got the repaired car on the way to Sioux City.

Brian Magee of the New York State DOT provided some important data on the condition of the state's roads in 1909.

Greg Miller is with the Local History Department of the Toledo-Lucas County Public Library, and was helpful in providing road information in the Toledo area.

Esther Mohnsen, a retired schoolmarm who lives in Leigh, Nebraska, is one brainy woman. She knew where she could lay her hands on a picture of the town's North-western Hotel for us.

Lillian Nellis and Kelly Farquhar, of the Montgomery County Historical Society, helped us out on the confusing route north of the Mohawk River.

Phil Notoriano's researcher, Alan Barnett, located Salt Lake City's post office in 1909 as well as the Knutsford Hotel. The Utah State Historical Society has a couple of good guys there.

Ellen Osborn, volunteering at the El Dorado County Museum in Placerville, Calif., did a lot of work searching for *Mountain Democrat* articles about Alice.

It was the wonderful Lincoln Highway researcher, Bob Owens, who found the article in the *Jefferson (Iowa) Bee* about Alice's passage through the town on her way to Carroll.

Joyce Pingleton, with the Lincoln County Library in Kemmerer, Wyoming, helped us out in our search for Alice's hotel in Opal.

Barbara Rabe lives in Wisner, Nebraska. Good thing she does, for she provided all the data of that town the night Alice stayed there, July 7, 1909.

Karen Buck Rennells has an extensive library of primary materials on her Buck Ranch and she knows how to use it. Karen, a friend for twenty years, has been a constant inspiration to this author. We asked for help in Opal—she not only provided the information, she found the photo, and she even told us that it's pronounced o-PAL.

Corrine Rickner and Betty Scheinost, best friends and great

237

researchers, live in Columbus, Nebraska. After getting some clues, Corrine was able to tell us exactly how Alice came through their town.

Somebody gave me the name of Gary Sides of Dakota City, Nebraska. I was told that if anybody would know where Alice stayed in Jackson, Nebraska, Gary would. He did.

Jerry Sides, Gary's dad, has driven the same roads Alice took from Denison to Sioux City, to Jackson, and to Wisner. He knew exactly where Alice left the road east of Crescent to turn south and enter Columbus.

Donald R. Snoddy, retired Union Pacific historian, knows every inch of the Chicago and Northwestern Railroad route, and how it followed the future Lincoln Highway in 1909. And he knew exactly where Alice's train crossed the Missouri River. A friend of more than twenty years, Don lives in Omaha.

We were nervous about writing that Alice boarded the Central Pacific to return to New Jersey, and we should have been—a check with Ed Strobridge, a noted railroad historian from San Luis Obispo, Calif., revealed that it was the Southern Pacific in 1909.

Leave it to Randy Wagner to come up with answers on the history of Wyoming. A past-president of the Lincoln Highway Association, he's the guy who located the site of the Inter-Ocean Hotel for me, and helped me out in so many other ways down through the years.

Michael E. Weigler, of Burlington, Wisc., was asked, "Do you happen to have a 1908 *Blue Book*, Mike?" "Sure do," he said. "Want to borrow it?" It's worth hundreds of dollars but he was willing. What a pal!

I doubt that anybody is more knowledgeable about the history of America's highway than Richard F. Weingroff. He works for the U.S. Department of Transportation, and what little he doesn't know he knows where to find. Smart cookie, and he helped a lot.

Those population figures for America's cities came from Nancy J. White, Population Division, U.S. Bureau of the Census. They came the day after I called for them.

So those are the helpers. If you like this book, raise your glass to them. I do.

—Gregory M. Franzwa
March 15, 2005

About the Author

Gregory M. Franzwa is the founder of both the Oregon-California Trails Association (1982) as well as the present Lincoln Highway Association (1992), and has received the highest awards for service to both organizations. He is the founding editor of the *Overland Journal,* the founding editor (and current editor) of the quarterly journal, *The Lincoln Highway Forum,* and is now in his eighteenth year as editor of *folio,* the quarterly journal of The Patrice Press. He is a graduate of the School of Journalism of the University of Iowa, a professional musician since the age of fourteen, and now heads the Old Pueblo Jazz Band. He and his wife, Kathy, live in Tucson, Arizona.

The 1909 Maxwell DA

Jesse G. Petersen and I are coauthors of the book, *The Lincoln Highway: Nevada*, Vol. 5 of a series of eleven. We were completing a book tour of this volume in the fall of 2004 with an appearance in Sparks, Nevada. After my talk, a fellow announced that a man was rebuilding a 1909 Maxwell DA, with the intention of replicating Alice Ramsey's trip in the centennial year, 2009. Sadly, I lacked the presence of mind to get the fellow's name.

I asked Geno Oliver to help. Geno is the Nevada director of the national Lincoln Highway Association. He tried, but it was a dead end. So I called Bob Lichty, retired director of the Canton (Ohio) Classic Car Museum. He didn't know either, but he referred me to Vern Campbell, who wrote back, "Yes, I know who this person is. He is Dr. Richard V. Anderson, of Monroe, Washington."

Rich replied to my plea for information on the very day I contacted him. He is indeed planning to have his car ready for a coast-to-coast trip by June 9, 2009, with his daughter, Emily Anderson, at the wheel.

Rich, 59 in early 2005, has been married to Margaret Anderson for thirty-five years. He earned a Ph.D. degree and has maintained a very successful private practice as a psychotherapist for the past thirty years. He's been collecting and restoring antique automobiles since 1968. Emily is single, a professional ski instructor, and currently coordinates the three-day program, "Walk for Breast Cancer," raising money for the Susan G. Koman Foundation.

I asked Rich to give our readers details of his project. Here is his response:

The car at present is completely apart, undergoing restoration, so it doesn't look like a car yet. But it will.

The engine appears to be nearing completion in this photo. Not so. We have a long way to go.

This is the front of the car, shown in our barn in the fall of 2004.

These photos appear to be very discouraging. Au contraire. This happens to be very exciting.

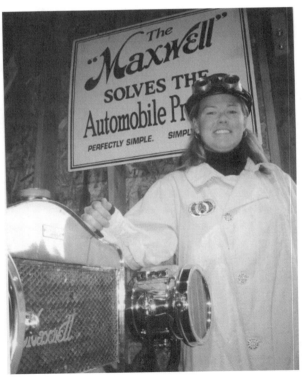

Emily Anderson in her duster, posing with a similar Maxwell.

First, I want to give credit to the late Tom Thoburn, of Ligonier, on the Lincoln Highway in western Pennsylvania. Tom and his wife, Tina, had wanted to take this trip for years. He had collected many parts for a Maxwell DA, and hoped to have Tina and probably his daughter, Teri Huston, do the drive in 2009. Teri and her husband, Ed, have been supportive in the restoration project. We lost Tom in 2003, but he gets the credit for getting so many of us fired up about the Maxwell automobile, and he made a very significant contribution to support Emily and me in doing this trip.

We'll be making replicas of those triangular pennants that can be seen in Alice's book, with the MBMC logo (for Maxwell-Briscoe Motor Club), and we'll have Tom's name embroidered on one. It will go to Tina after the trip. We hope Tina and Teri can ride with us part of the way.

We got our car from Sterling Walsh, who lives near Baltimore, who has the only other 1909 DA in existence. He's allowed us to photograph his car, get dimensions, and copy parts. He's owned his DA for forty-five years, and got a lot a lot of parts from Tom Thoburn. Sterling loans parts to me whenever I need them, makes engineering drawings and diagrams of other parts for me.

Work on our car started in October 2004, in hopes that it can be done by June 2008. That will give us a year to get rid of any bugs and make it solidly road worthy by June 9, 2009.

Many parts have been sandblasted and primed, and right now a painter is finishing the chassis, fenders, and some other parts. The front axle has been completely restored with new bearings. The hubs and spindles are all fitted now. We are about ready to start having new wood wheels made. New springs are now being fabricated, and we should have our new tires soon.

All cars of Alice's era were equipped with tubed tires with no tread on the fabric covering. We have learned that such tires today last only about 1,000 miles, so we have ordered Goodrich Silvertown cords—black and pretty beefy—and they should last the entire trip and then some.

Parts like wheels and springs, so critical for safety, are being made new, to the precise specifications of the originals.

Engine restoration hasn't begun, but it will be a model rebuild, complete right down to every single nut and bolt. New rings in the pistons, cylinders honed (but not bored any bigger), all bearings redone, and the whole transmission rebuilt, with new clutch disks. It will be essentially like the original, but we're going to have to cheat in a couple of areas. Our DA will be built for the trip, not for a museum.

First, there will be a different distributor system, with electronic ignition concealed within the distributor. That will allow the engine to be started easier, and it should run better as well.

Also, I'll build it with dual ignition—two sets of spark plugs instead of one, and that should eliminate the possibility of misfiring. We'll keep the valves the same, but we'll probably add two-cycle oil to regular gasoline, to keep the intake valves lubricated. Today's low-octane gas sometimes causes valves in engines like this to run dry and stick.

I know that, like Alice Ramsey, we probably will be getting to some of the scheduled stops after dark. We'll have the same type of carbide lamps up front, but I'm thinking of concealing halogen bulbs in the headlamp housings. Most folks wouldn't notice this.

I have some good friends in Sacramento, Tim and Barb Simonsma. Tim is a Maxwell mechanic and a retired heavy equipment mechanic as well. He wants to put the Maxwell in his enclosed car carrier and tow it to New York behind his motor home. And he wants to follow the Maxwell on its daily runs, securing it inside the trailer every night. Tim and all his tools will be along to do whatever needs to be done along the way to keep the DA on the road, and prepping it every night for the next day's run.

Gregory M. Franzwa has offered to give us all the research he has performed in developing the annotation for Alice's Drive, and especially the "Chasing Alice" section of his book. We won't be able to drive Alice Ramsey's precise routes, for many of those roads are now on private property, or simply no longer exist. But we'll come close.

As those who have read Alice Ramsey's book know, her husband gave her a new 1908 Maxwell Model K runabout, in which she learned to drive. In an incredible piece of luck, I found a 1908 K in a barn in Canton, Ohio—with enough paint and upholstery to know that it is identical to Alice's runabout—red finish with red upholstery. As far as I know, it is the only 1908 K known to exist.

We're making this trip for many reasons, the first and foremost being it will be a lot of fun. But it will also call attention to how far our civilization has come in transportation—both in automobiles and in highways. Also, we want to honor the memory of Alice Ramsey, a courageous and highly skilled young woman.

And finally, since we will be on the historic Lincoln Highway for two-thirds of the way, we hope to promote the ideals of the current Lincoln Highway Association—the awareness of its route, an awareness which will lead to its preservation. That, more than anything else, is worth the effort.

—Richard V. Anderson
Monroe, Washington
March 2005

INDEX

Index

Index

Glidden, Iowa, 140
Glidden, Joseph F., 52, 55n
Gnehm, Eugene, 73, 74-75, 77
Gold Discovery State Historic Park,
Calif., 134n
gold rush, California, 230
Golden Gate (Calif.), 11
Goodale, Will, 92, 94-95
Goodyear Tire & Rubber Co., 19
Goshen, Ind., 40, 43n, 167
Gothenburg, Nebr., 195-196
Gothenburg Stairstep, 195
Government Creek Bridge, 217
Grand Island, Nebr., 81-83, 195
Granger, Wyo., 104n, 210-211
Grantsville, Utah, 109, 215
Great Depression, 21n
Great Lakes, 40
Great Salt Lake, 108-109, 214
Great Salt Lake Desert, 108-109
Green River, Wyo., 104n, 210
Greenbush Bridge, Old, 29n, 155
Groves, H. B., 73, 74-77

Haag family, Jefferson, Iowa, 68, 186-187
Haag, Pauline, 68
Hackensack, N.J., 3-4, 16, 21n, 22n, 34, 141, 178
Hackensack Brick Co., 141
Hackensack, N.J., Woman's Club of, 21n
Halstead's Bazaar (Hackensack, N.J.), 16
Hamilton, Nev., 221
Hammond, Ind., 1, 44n
Handley, Mr., 41, 45
Hangtown (Placerville), Calif., 130
Harlem River, 9n, 144
Harper, Wyo., 205

Hascall Hotel, 43n, 167
Hathaway, Al, 55n
Hathaway, W. S., 72
Haynes automobile, 19
Hayward, Calif., 131, 134n, 230-231
Hayward's Hotel, Hayward, Calif., 231
Hazen, Nev., 123
Heilbron, Louise, 130
Hell Gate, 11, 21n, 133
Henderson, Ashton Marvin, 140
Henry Hudson Parkway, 9n
Herkimer, N.Y., 158
Herring Hotel, 63, 65n, 184-185
Hershey, Nebr., 197
Hill, Clare, 83
Hill, W. H., 83-84
Hillsdale, Wyo., 104n
Hine, C. G., 145, 146, 150, 153, 154
Hiner, D. A., 57-58
Hollenden Hotel, 39, 43n, 162-164
Hollingsworth Hotel, Ogallala, Nebr., 197
Holmes, T. F., 126
Hoesley, Mr., 80
Homer, Nebr. 193
Honey Creek, Iowa, 187
Hope, Bob, 180
horns, musical, 164
Howell, Wyo., 205
Howells, Nebr., 80, 90n, 194
Hub, The, restaurant, 28, 30n
Hudson, N.Y., 153
Hudson River, 6, 22n, 26, 29n, 141, 145, 150, 154
Hull, Arthur, 131
Huyler, Ada, 141
Huyler, John, 8n
Hyde Park, N.Y., 24, 29n
Hynds Building, 104n, 203

Index

253

THE LINCOLN HIGHWAY ASSOCIATION

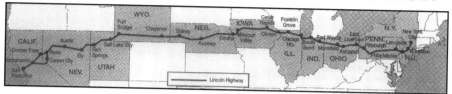

The new Lincoln Highway Association was founded Oct. 31, 1992, for the express purpose of saving endangered sections of the old Lincoln Highway. To that end the LHA has been effective, but much more remains to be done to end the ongoing threats to the great highway.

Membership in the LHA is vitally important, for as the organization has proved, there is indeed strength in numbers. In addition to the satisfaction of knowing that you are helping save the historic highway, to be enjoyed by your children and grandchildren, there are many benefits to membership.

Each member is automatically enrolled in a state chapter, and those chapters have many interesting activities each year. There are tours of the old Lincoln Highway, often in classic cars, as well as meetings in historic structures along the road. Each year members also receive four issues of *The Lincoln Highway Forum,* containing articles of great interest, usually written by the members. All LHA members also receive a roster of the membership, complete with e-mail addresses, and a handsome cloisonné lapel pin of the historic Lincoln Highway logo *(right),* adopted in 1914.

Four-day conventions are held during the second week of June each year in Lincoln Highway states. Activities include two days of bus tours, east and west of the highway, a welcoming reception, numerous lectures and slide shows, a book room where members can purchase Lincoln Highway books and souvenirs, and view memorabilia and postcard collections containing thousands of items. Although the educational activities during the conferences are important, most members derive a lot of joy out of the camaraderie. Old hands always help the new members feel welcome.

Call the toll-free number of The Patrice Press for a membership application, 1/800/367-9242; or access the LHA's website: http://www.lincolnhighwayassoc.org.This connects you with the membership desk in our national headquarters, in the H. I. Lincoln building in Franklin Grove, Illinois.

The LHA has been given tax-deductible status, through section 501(c)(3) of the Internal Revenue code.

ENROLL IN THE LINCOLN HIGHWAY SUBSCRIPTION SERIES

Our state-by-state series on the Lincoln Highway started with Vol. 1, *The Lincoln Highway: Iowa,* and now includes *The Lincoln Highway: Nebraska; The Lincoln Highway: Wyoming; The Lincoln Highway: Utah;* and *The Lincoln Highway: Nevada. The Lincoln Highway: California* should be in print in 2005.

Then we'll start researching and writing *The Lincoln Highway: Illinois,* and continue with the states east of there, concluding with *The Lincoln Highway: New York-New Jersey.*

Series subscribers realize a savings of $5 per book, on the cloth-bound hardcover edition (below left); or $15 per book on the volume bound in top grain genuine leather. (The signed and numbered leather edition is limited to fifteen subscribers; there are eleven subscribers currently.)

Series subscribers enter into a non-binding agreement to buy the entire series. As soon as a manufacturer announces a ship date for each new volume, subscribers are notfied by mail and asked to validate their order, and if appropriate update their credit card information. The credit cards are not debited until the book is sent to the subscriber. The subscriber may terminate the agreement at any time with no penalty. Those who wish to subscribe must have all the earlier volumes.

To enroll as a series subscriber, notify us by email (books@patrice press.com), fax (1/520/743-7034), or call our toll-free line (1/800/367-9242). Checks, Visa or MasterCard are accepted, or we can bill—your choice.

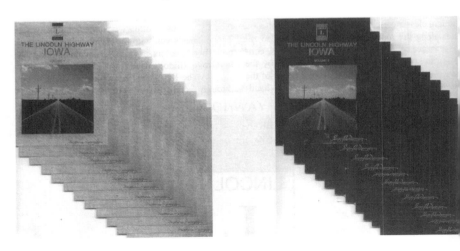